GREEN

*A reflection on love and loss through
a lifetime relationship with the land*

A COLLECTION OF SHORT STORIES
BY DAN TAWCZYNSKI

Stories written by Dan Tawczynski

Cover Illustration by Maggie Fricke

Published by Farmer Dan, LLC
Great Barrington, Massachusetts

ISBN 978-0-578-90267-8

Library of Congress Control Number: 2021909130

Light of the Moon, Inc.
Partnering with self-published authors since 2009
Book Design/Production/Consulting
Carbondale, Colorado • www.lightofthemooninc.com

Dedication

In the introduction to this work, I mention three individuals whose influence helped me chart the course of my life at critical times. By no means were they the only ones. This book is dedicated to those individuals as well as the family, neighbors, employees, and even customers that kept me going when at times it seemed there was no way to continue.

Table of Contents

Introduction

As the seasons inevitably descend through the autumn of my years, necessity forces me to hand off responsibilities that were once mine alone. The time has come to pass the torch, or maybe the hoe. Friends, associates, and even sometimes family ask why I stayed with farming when so many opportunities to financially advance came and went. I could have gone in other directions, even after the choice had been made, and was occasionally tempted by attractive, sometimes substantial offers. I could be a wealthy man today, and I am, though my wallet often suffers stress.

I can't say moving on hasn't crossed my mind. Lucrative opportunities have had a way of presenting themselves at times when they are most difficult to resist. Any farmer is tempted when winter seems to go on forever and the growing pile of unpaid bills gnaws at your soul. Longer light and warmer temperatures do arrive eventually. Nothing compares with spring fever on a farm. A few sunny days, the buds of life bursting forth and restoring a spark of life even to the most weary of souls. When weakened by a seemingly relentless depression, in spring one can find a smile and new determination. There is nothing so intoxicating as the perfume of freshly turned fertile soil. Perhaps it's the promise that "this will be the year..."

In the past, good fortune has somehow found a way to smile on me whenever I found myself approaching a major crossroad. Often the guiding signpost revealed itself in the form of the right individual who just happened by to help me make the proper decision, whether he realized it or not. The least likely encounters tend to leave the deepest impressions. When I was a child, maybe only six or seven years old, an elderly neighbor gave me words to live by. Some might remember Harry Rahm as the man who always picked his sweet corn before the Fourth of July. I have yet to accomplish this feat even once despite farming some of the same ground. Mr. Rahm was regarded by most adults as somewhat of a curmudgeonly character, but I always thought of him as a wise elder. He told me the best fertilizer for a field was a good, sincere smile. If you were having a bad day it was best to stay away. He must have smiled a lot. He was the most successful grower I have ever known.

In the spring of 1955, when I was ten, my mother and father split up, a nasty separation that left deep scars on my young mind. I don't know if adults realize what happens to a child when his world is destroyed. Perhaps if they understood they would find a way to inflict less pain on those they claim to love. Two things saved me from going insane: my dog and my gardens. My dog sensed trouble and was never far from my side, and working the soil gave me a healing no human contact could compete with.

I was entering high school when another epiphany occurred through a man I only knew as Fred, a kindly gent I conversed with almost weekly as he came to retrieve his equally elderly wife from the clutches of her hairdresser, my mother. By this time, my summer job was almost four acres of garden, the results of which I sold from a small roadside market. From planting and growing to harvest and sales I did everything, often under conditions less than desirable. If I didn't do it, it didn't get done, no matter what it was. While my friends were swimming and playing ball, and later doing what teenagers did, I worked my gardens.

One particularly hot day in late June, Fred worked his way out to where I was hoeing potatoes. On in his years, he needed a cane in each hand, arthritis and an old injury having taken the inevitable toll. After required small talk about the ungodly heat, he asked what I was intending to study in college, since he'd heard this was why I kept the gardens.

"Engineering," was my prompt reply. The Russians had been launching Sputniks and the president had called for a mobilization in the sciences. I had always designed and built my own model aircraft and crude rockets, a pastime my business was sometimes forced to compete with. I viewed becoming an engineer as an avenue toward making my hobby into a career.

"No," Fred replied. "You're going to be a farmer. Any engineer would find a way to not work in this heat. He'd make an excuse. You know what work is ... regardless."

I progressed through high school, taking all the advanced math and science courses offered but I kept up the farming. If anything, my little farm increased in size, mostly because it held promise of a revenue stream to help with future expenses. But by the time I was ready for college, world events and the military-industrial relationship President Eisenhower had warned about tipped my engineering switch into the "off" position. A high school teacher taught me to be more analytical than accepting. He encouraged me to make decisions based on observation and research, not just what I was told. Fighting a war in Asia made no sense to me. Not wanting to become another cog in this wheel, I gravitated to the arts and eventually graduated with an English degree and teaching certificate.

I took a job as a junior high English instructor and found myself teaching a lot more than grammar and literature. My curriculum was based on what I felt kids needed to know, especially about a war in a place where many would lose their innocence, some their lives. The approved courses were irrelevant to youth sometimes considered disposable by their elders. I taught two how to tell time on an analog clock, others how to use a phone book. No one had ever bothered. More than once this approach put me in hot water, but all I could think about was Falstaff's line of, "Cannon fodder, sire ... cannon fodder." I would return to the farm after school and take my frustrations out on weeds and pests because I knew many of my students would be swept up in the draft. You know, I had never given it much thought but one of the reasons I chose teaching was that it permitted me to remain a farmer in the summer. The farm was saving my sanity. Completely burned out by futility, I left the teaching profession after a little more than three years to pursue the farm full-time.

Revulsion at war and world politics may have been a reason not to pursue engineering, but Fred had been right; my release from personal tension was the good earth. To this day when heavy thinking is on the agenda, I pick up a hoe or rake, or some other tool, and work the soil to pull weeds or nurse a struggling plant. I must get closer to the earth to take advantage of the therapy fertile ground has always offered.

Years passed all too quickly; my business grew like Topsy, the KISS (Keep it Simple Stupid) principle long since violated, and yet another remarkable individual left his mark. Bill Cole was a native New Hampshirite, a rugged individualist by any definition, and a jack-of-all-trades. He always had a kind word and friendly smile, never looking to find fault. He was also one of the most intelligent people I have ever met, a near-genius uncorrupted by formal education.

It was a particularly busy day at the store, and my whole family was helping. My wife was in the kitchen, two daughters out front with the customers, and Keith, then almost fifteen, sweating in the field with a corn-picking crew. Six-year-old Paul amused himself playing in the small stream that flowed near the store. He knew better than to bother the rest of us, and no matter how dirty he could get there was always a bath before bed.

Business bordered on insanity; it was one of those days when if everything went well you might find a way to pay a few bills. I was being pulled in a dozen directions when a female scream pierced the din. My little one was showing a fashionably dressed woman from the city the giant bullfrog he had just caught. I don't know whether the woman was screaming about the frog or my son. He was dirty, as though he had been cleaning a furnace or playing in crude oil. I never knew dirt could stick to anyone the way he was wearing it.

Customers reacted as if a mass murder was taking place, and I was about to lose everything when Bill laughed and uttered profound words of wisdom: "You know, there just ain't no better place to bring up kids than on a farm."

The customers got over their initial fright and started laughing. Soap and water, a lot of both, would clean up the child and shortly the frog was safely returned to the stream. But more importantly, I was shown another reason why this way of life was so precious. At one time it had been all about me, my dreams and my goals, but now the only thing that really mattered was being a good parent and doing what was best for my family.

Life on the land is a good thing, with a generous helping of hard work and stress thrown in for flavor; it is without doubt the best any child can hope for. If I had gone to work for some mega-corporation, living in the city or even the suburbs, could my children have ever had the experience, the appreciation for food, the learning about life that comes from a farm? Could I have lived with myself and my family knowing that I was just adding to the wealth of some nameless individuals that already had more money than they or their offspring could ever spend?

Harry, Fred, and Bill have all gone on to their rewards, but the lessons learned from each remain forever. The Shakers had it right. "Nothing is so profound as simplicity."

A few times in my life, I have been privileged to witness a phenomenon I have yet to adequately describe. It can occur at any time in the growing season but most often in June, when the days are longest, that time of the year when on a warm night you can hear the corn grow. For no apparent reason you find yourself surrounded by a kind of green mist, a vaporous substance defying description. It envelops and swirls about you seemingly with a mind of its own. I thought I was going crazy at first but when it happened again, and a third time, I knew better.

Any person is a changed individual after experiencing what I can only call an Earth Miracle. One time my mother and father, now reconciled, were with me when it occurred. They both said they felt a rapture but could not explain it. It was like seeing God and receiving validation that what you are doing is the right thing.

Years ago, I wrote about this phenomenon in a letter to a local newspaper. Several farmers responded that on occasion they'd been witness to the phenomenon as well. One woman wrote she had experienced it with her father who had seen it with his father. A national agricultural magazine picked up the story, and I received letters from all over farm country, many saying, "I didn't want to say anything because people would think I was going nuts."

I'm convinced that you must be a farmer to see that color green. No artist can capture it. Poets find themselves inadequate. The words do not exist. The closest most similar event I've ever witnessed was on the plains of Africa the day after the rains came. What was brown and dry suddenly became lush and alive in a matter of hours, a transformation nothing short of miraculous.

If there is a God, He speaks to me and others through that green mist, that corn, and we receive validation for what we've chosen as our life's work. That green mist and that green corn are greener than the back of any dollar bill I've ever held in my hand.

When someone asks me why I keep farming despite the hardships, I just smile. I am the wealthiest person I know.

Childhood Memories

Fishing with Mitzie

I was a ten-year-old kid with parents at each other's throats, time on my hands, and few places to go. My mother and father, now legally divorced, lived little more than a quarter of a mile apart, saw each other almost daily (from a distance), and used me as a conduit to express their dislike of one another pretty much just as often.

It was up to me to visit Dad since the law said I had to live with Mom. No visitation standards were ever established since they lived in such proximity, so if I didn't visit enough it was my fault. The fact that I was a kid who had just learned how to ride a bike (I had won it at the Barrington Fair) and often had to make these visits after dark didn't seem to make a difference. Neither noticed that I needed to have a childhood. Sports, Little League and such, became a luxury rather than a normal activity, and both seemed to take pains to make me understand how much they were sacrificing to allow me these activities. Any time I could steal to be alone, to be a child, to do the things kids expected was an exception, not the rule.

It is said a man's best friend is his dog. I am older now and have to say it's even more of a truism when you're a kid. I could list the names and the kinds of dogs that have owned me, but the obvious truth is they are your best friends at any time in your life.

Perhaps recognizing a brewing problem a few months after the split, my mother took me to a local dairy farm where there was a litter of puppies—heritage unknown—to be given away. I remember at least ten young pups playing and I was told to take my pick. The runt of the litter came over and licked my hand. There was no way to resist as the others continued playing with each other while maintaining distance.

Because of her white paws we called her Mitzie. Mom said we named her after Mitzie Gaynor the actress. I didn't care. She loved me and I loved her. Mitzie never whined, even during the first night she was away from her mother. She greeted me every morning and waited patiently for me every day until the school bus arrived. A built-in time clock guided her to within a few minutes of when I would be home.

Because dogs were not allowed in the house, Mitzie slept under the window of my bedroom outside in the flowerbed. No matter what Mom did to deter the dog, Mitzie slept as close to me as she could. That was the flowerbed. Large rocks were somehow moved, stakes pulled out, for the dog was determined. I confess, she had help, and eventually Mom caved in. Mitzie slept where she wanted to. The weather had no influence on her devotion, especially in her younger years. As she got older, it took temperature of below zero to make her go sleep in the hay in the barn. As she aged, the basement became available with a ready blanket. Mitzie never once made a mess in the house—not as a puppy or as a senior citizen. She always found a way to let you know her needs, and somehow, if you were slow to respond, she held it.

Despite all her outstanding habits, the one thing that stands out most in my memory was her unbounded devotion. Whenever I was home that dog was with me. If I was working in the garden, bicycling off to go swimming, fishing, or just roaming around the woods near home, she was with me.

Fishing was my release from the family tension, and whenever and wherever I went Mitzie was alongside me. I remember Mom saying she never worried because she knew Mitzie would take care of me.

For her size Mitzie was the most ferocious creature on the planet. No animal stood a chance at causing me harm. Fear was not something this dog registered. Humans she could tolerate, though she watched closely, sometimes uttering a low bark. But no animal could ever think of getting close, wherever I might be. Smaller animals, like mice, were sport for her, digging and sniffing them out, but I personally saw her take on and kill raccoons, opossums, squirrels (when she could catch them), and woodchucks in numbers I can only estimate. At about thirty pounds or so, some of her prey outweighed her but none was as fearless. This dog did not know how to be afraid, and there were times it cost her, especially with porcupines. More than once she came home with quills all over her face, but the next time the porcupine would be dead on the front lawn. This scene played out every summer. I had to get rid of at least a dozen dead porcupines in the years Mitzie was with me, not to mention woodchucks, squirrels, chipmunks, muskrats and raccoons that were too many to count. Yes, this little dog killed many raccoons. I never had damage to my sweet corn when Mitzie was around.

Whenever she suffered quills in her face, she would come up to me with a mournful look. The most she ever did was give a little yip each time I extracted a quill, but she knew I was only trying to help and never made the job any more difficult than it had to be. She knew what had to be done and put up with it. Curiously, if I missed one, she let me know by not lapping up the milk I would put in her bowl and instead staying close, insisting I take another look. If I missed one it was always in her mouth and painful to remove, but she always let me do it, licking my hand before she drank the milk.

Other than quills I only remember one time she was ever injured by another animal, and that, ironically, was by a mouse. Like many farm dogs she enjoyed digging after field mice. It was almost funny to watch because after a concerted effort to dig out their burrows they would make a jailbreak, running in all directions, thoroughly confusing the dog. As often as not, they all got away. But once a mouse took exception to Mitzie excavating his burrow. Dogs will dig for a while and then take a long hard sniff to determine which direction to continue the dig. There were at least a half-dozen digs and long sniffs. Mitzie was digging and sniffing but still no mice. Then it happened. When

Mitzie pushed her nose in as far as she could to take another sniff, I heard a yelp and she pulled back, mad as hell. Firmly attached to the tip of her nose was a rather large field mouse. Maybe this was one that had been dug out before, I don't know, but unlike its fellow mice, it decided to go out in a blaze of glory. She howled with pain as she peeled the creature off her nose and dispatched it. Her nose was bleeding, but she would not let me treat her. The rest of the mice in the burrow easily escaped. I think she was embarrassed by what happened and decided to show us who really ruled the kingdom. For the next two weeks there wasn't a day that went by without some animal she had caught lying on the front lawn. I know because Mom made me bury them all. Nothing like a dead woodchuck lying near the doorstep to encourage business in her hair salon.

The thing that set Mitzie apart from any other dog was her unquestioned love and devotion, especially when I needed it the most. She was able to sense if anything was wrong and would press closer when I needed it.

I'm hesitant to attach blame to my family situation, for I was just caught in the middle. When frustration built to an intolerable level, I went fishing, with Mitzie. I had my choice of places, a good thing because if I needed to be alone there was no one place I could be found, and I could have peace until either someone located me or I chose to go home. I would catch and release most fish, sometimes bringing a few home for the barn cats, and Mitzie was always there.

On occasion, I just laid down in the tall grass by the river and tried to get my head straight, not even getting my line wet, and without fail Mitzie was by my side, feeling my confusion and pain and showing nothing but unconditional love. I think I said more to that dog than I said to either of my parents during that incomprehensible period in my life. There were times she understood better than either of them. If I can be regarded as sane today it is only because of that dog. She never judged, never found fault, and never made me seem unworthy of any windfall that came my way. Mitzie was always there, never failing.

Mom told me that while I was away in Michigan, at St. Mary's, Mitzie just followed her around, showing little interest in anything; even her hunting ceased. When I came home for Christmas, Easter, or summer vacation, Mitzie came alive. When I had to return to school, I found it hardest to say goodbye to her. There was a bond between us no other could understand. She knew more about me than any human and never questioned or doubted. On these occasions I cried, and I think she did as well.

While I was away at Orchard Lake, things gradually improved between Mom and Dad, but when I came home on vacation no one greeted me more lovingly than Mitzie. I began to wonder if in my absence Mitzie's love was having a desirable effect on Mom and Dad as well. By the time I graduated and started to prepare for college, they were almost reconciled, though still living a quarter mile apart. I swear Mitzie was responsible. Whenever I was home she was with me, but when I was gone she split her time between the two of them, or at least that's what I was told. Dad worked in town during the day and Mom worked in her hairdresser's shop attached to the house. Mitzie greeted Dad in the evening. Mom said Mitzie accompanied her whenever she did the chores (we had animals) both morning and evening. Mitzie always seemed to be there; splitting her time between two people a quarter mile apart was no problem. She had the same effect on both, knowing the problem, and taking what could only be called affirmative action.

In 1964, we had not one but two devastating fires, events that changed lives forever. This was the summer between my freshman and sophomore years at Boston College. Toward the end of the term, I had summoned up my nerve and finally asked Martha out on a date, a Red Sox game. It was like a bolt of lightning hit. We were madly in love from the start and we both knew it. We wrote long letters to one another on an almost daily basis after parting for the summer.

On July the first we had a violent thunderstorm and our barn was struck by lightning. Cattle, hay, machinery—just about everything was lost. Ironically, to say the least, my brother Stan worked for a company that installed lightning rods. They had come out, given an estimate, and we gave the go-ahead. They showed up to do the installation the morning after the barn was struck. Talk about being a day late and a dollar short.

Mitzie had been in the barn when the lightning struck, seeking shelter from the hail and rain. I knew something was wrong when I saw her running for the house to her place beneath my bedroom window at the height of the storm. The barn was obscured from view, but by the time I had seen what happened the whole thing was engulfed in flames. We had been bringing in hay just before the storm hit and were patting ourselves on the back for getting it just in time. The last load, still on the wagon, and the tractor that pulled it there were visible—in flames—just inside the door. There wasn't a damn thing we could do. I remember the sounds of animals screaming (they do scream, believe me, at least when they are forced to die slowly and in incredible pain) and the feeling of total helplessness.

Digging big holes and burying a dozen animals that were calling out to you, their master and protector, to save them only hours ago was more than difficult. Every cow and calf had a name, and most answered to them. We were not saying goodbye to animals, but friends. They had depended on us and we had failed. Through everything, all the agony possible to imagine, Mitzie was never more than a few feet away. She had a duty to perform, and that duty was me.

Martha and I, in conjunction with our families, had scheduled a visit that occurred less than a week after the fire. We talked on the phone many times in the interim, and we both decided we had to see one another despite what had happened. Mitzie was with me when I picked up Martha at the bus stop. She knew there was something different between Martha and me. Martha, to Mitzie, was like an extension of me: guard her and love her. This human was special.

Mitzie accompanied us as I drove Martha back to the bus stop for her return trip. I was scheduled to make a journey to New Jersey in a couple of weeks. Little doubt existed between us, though more was to transpire before things came together. We both said our goodbyes, me with a kiss and Mitzie with a lick of the hand.

But there was another fly in the ointment. Two weeks to the day after the first fire I was asked to drive a carload of youngsters down to the World's Fair in New York for a priest, a family friend. I get the strong feeling, in retrospect, that he invited me along more as a guest in view of what our family had gone through. In any case I drove a group of largely unruly altar boys and others to what would have to be considered a once-in-a-lifetime experience.

I had a hard time fighting off fatigue on the late-night return to the Berkshires. At one point I was the only one still awake in the car, though not by much. Everyone else was fast asleep. The priest friend, Father John, after having had at least a little rest directed me to head to my home. He would take care of the drop-offs.

As I turned up Division Street, I caught sight of a figure in the driveway of my mother's house. It was Dad, waving us to a stop—most unusual at three in the morning.

"Don't pull in, Danny. Go to your sister's across the street. There's been another fire, this time it's the house."

Standing next to him was Mitzie.

The extreme fatigue combined with the devastating news was about all I could take. I put my head down and I cried. Mitzie came to my side and licked my face. No matter what could or would happen, she was my best friend. Mitzie was not allowed in my sister's house, but for the rest of that sleepless night she laid by the door keeping watch. Just before daybreak she sounded the alarm; headlights had pulled in across the street. We all jumped up and ran after the dog who was not going to let an intruder get anywhere near our home. Turned out it was a friend, a local policeman, just checking that all was okay. Once assured he was not a threat, Mitzie licked his hand, asking forgiveness. Any other dog would have attacked.

This had to be one of the lowest points of my life. I had been planning to visit Martha in Montclair, New Jersey in a week but now everything was totally upset. My return to Boston College in the fall was seriously in doubt. Financially, the family was in dire straits since the hair salon my mother operated was burned out, and the animals were lost. Dad had retired and was now living on social security. What would we do?

For most of the rest of the summer, the sole source of income for the family was the produce I was selling from the fields as we worked at putting our lives back together. We reached a settlement with our insurance company and almost immediately work began on restoring the house and beauty salon. A neighbor who was also a building contractor offered to help us with a barn if we worked with him. A local sawmill offered lumber with generous terms (he had been burned out himself a few years earlier) and at least we could see the beginnings of hope.

I made the pilgrimage down to see Martha, got the introduction to her family, perhaps not making the best of impressions but, under the circumstances, not doing that badly. I brought them sweet corn, the likes of which they had not tasted in years, and somehow assured them I had nothing but the best of intentions with their daughter.

When I returned home, I still had to confront the issue of returning to college. I never worked so hard and slept so little in my life. I told myself that no matter what happened, my family— which had now come together again—was first and foremost.

Stan was able to locate another tractor and equipment for a price, and while he spent time rebuilding the one that had been in the fire, I was able to bring in hay for the remaining animals, help with the rebuilding of the barn, and grow, harvest, and sell more produce than ever. Bit by bit the picture pieced itself back together. There were times when tempers became short, brought on by extreme fatigue, but somehow we survived. I even managed to get in most of the required summer reading.

Loans and student aid were not something we even considered. I'm sure we would have qualified for at least some help but my mother and father, both having lived through the Depression years, were leery of taking out any loan. If we were going to do this, and Dad said we were, we were going to do it on our own.

Boston College had a very bad practice of sending out tuition and other bills just before you were due to arrive back on campus, leaving little to no time to mail back payment. A family friend once told me it cost her almost a hundred dollars in fees just to make sure the payment got there in time for her son's return. The bill came in the mail and we had a family meeting. We made it work, at least for this semester.

It was even harder to say goodbye to Mitzie this time. She was getting on in her years, not many left for her, but she had been at my side through the toughest of times. She knew I would be home most weekends, as there was just so much to do that I couldn't afford to stay in Boston and fool around. Others had made sacrifices; the least I could do was help when I could.

Just before Thanksgiving break, I saw a note on the bulletin board by the financial aid office saying the Metropolitan Transportation Authority was looking for emergency (read, temporary) workers to help with snow removal at Logan Airport, class II driver's license preferred. I had a class II truck driver's license, and since Boston College was mostly a commuter school at the time, if there was a snow emergency classes were cancelled—a perfect fit.

Other guys who came from working class backgrounds and I showed up en masse at the opportunity. I had been handling farm equipment since the age of six, though I had never driven anything as large as a Walter Sno-fighter. I showed them I knew what it was about and was told to be on stand-by whenever I heard a storm was coming. That season I think Boston set a record for the greatest number of "Nor-Easters," and I never missed a class because I was working. The match was perfect, and I very nearly earned my tuition for the next semester. With a little help from Mom and Dad the second semester was assured.

I had to keep an eye out for the next storm and stay at the campus when the potential to be called in to work existed, but I did manage to get home on occasion, and the first one to greet me was Mitzie. In her advanced years (she was at least eleven by then) Mom allowed her to spend nights in the basement. She had a nice bed and it was warm down there, having been finished off after the fire. It was the only place we had to live while the house was being rebuilt and remained the family focal point thereafter. Her bed was near the fireplace and she was comfortable, though she did little hunting other than the occasional mouse, and sometimes the mouse was ignored.

Every time I came home, sometimes with Martha now, she greeted us, not just me anymore. She was on her way out and she knew it. But there were important things to be taken care of whenever we showed up. It was as if her aging could be put on hold for the weekend, but not for much longer. One weekend as Martha and I walked in the door, Mom handed me Mitzie's collar … I think I felt worse for the loss of that dog than I have for the deaths of people I have known.

I can fully understand what makes a person, especially a child, go over the edge if a series of traumatic events overtakes them. The rock, the foundation called family, had been ripped from beneath me at a vulnerable age. I felt that neither of my parents wanted or loved me anymore. My very existence had become a problem for both, a tool, a way for each to wreak havoc on the other. I was not stupid; I could see what was going on but was powerless to do anything about it. For those terrible rough years, the best and often only friend I had was Mitzie.

I have never had a bad dog; they have all been good and highly devoted, especially the enormous Newfoundland, Muffin, who keeps company with me now. But no dog ever meant more to me, kept me at least pretending to be sane at a time when all forces seemed arrayed against remaining rational, and guided me to a better life. If there is a heaven for either humans or dogs, Mitzie is there, watching for the occasional mouse, waiting for me, and she knows where the big fish are biting.

My Little Brook

Dad taught me how to fish in '49. I was a little over four years old and I wished I could have spent all day, every day with him. He was God; he knew everything, and I wanted to learn.

After he had come home from work, done various chores around the house, and we all had supper together, he would magically find a can of worms and a couple of fishing rods (primitive, by today's standards) and we would walk the two hundred yards to where the bridge had washed out in the famous New Year's Flood of '48–49.

Though the channel has changed somewhat, the abutment we fished from is still there. He showed me how to bait a hook, to use a cork from a wine bottle as a bobber, and to be patient while waiting for a bite. We caught lots of sunfish; I never knew there were so many kinds and colors: perch, bullhead, bass, and others—species I haven't seen since.

The Housatonic River was even then regarded as polluted, so we never kept anything to eat, but we always saved a few for the family of cats we had back home. Cats were essential if you kept animals, and grain to feed them. It was the only way to control rodents. The cats would come running as we entered the yard. Fish was a treat for the cats, so we always made sure we had at least one for each.

The great flood, one of my earliest memories, changed the landscape of the area on a mega-scale. I remember all of us kids from the neighborhood with our parents taking a major walk of exploration the spring after. Piles of debris from upstream clogged what were once farm roads. Holes in the ground were either filled in with new deposit or were scoured out to make new canyons, or in some cases, new ponds.

A former backwater just below the Rising Paper Mill became isolated from the rest of the river. Someone, I'm not sure who, declared the fish from here were safe to eat. Each Sunday afternoon, after all the chores were completed, the neighborhood kids, along with assorted responsible adults, would walk en masse to this backwater to catch a few perch and bullheads for supper. It was more about the camaraderie and friendship than the fish, but as a kid you had to have done something really bad to be punished by not being allowed to go. This was the highlight of the week and we all more than looked forward to it.

On the way, a walk of perhaps a little more than a half-mile, the path led us past a small pond scooped out by the floodwaters. Numerous Bluegill and Sunfish fought over the occasional worm thrown to tempt them but a larger, more secretive fish kept his distance. Despite the various methods we tried, even the adults, nothing caused this fish to stir. It stayed off to the side where it was least vulnerable and watched as many of its pond-mates were hauled off to become cat food.

Our house was the closest to both the backwater and this little pond, still visible in part to this very day, though mostly filled in by a graveling operation. My five-year-old mind knew every inch of the area. This was my world. I would dig myself a few worms and take my child-sized rod from the shed and walk the quarter-mile or so to the little pond. It had become my mission to catch that mystery fish.

In those days, there was not as much concern about a little boy off on his own as there is today. It wasn't until many years later I found out that on almost every occasion someone was watching, just to make sure I didn't get into trouble. It wasn't long before they figured out where I was going and made sure I got there safely, not that there was anything to be worried about. I wasn't hard to follow or track; they just had to listen to the singing. "How much is that doggie in the window," or

"Mockingbird Hill." I sang at the top of my lungs, not a care in the world, but the world listened and smiled on a little boy with his fishing rod.

Almost daily I would search for worms, find my rod, and head for the little pond. Just as often I would see the mystery fish head for cover as soon as I appeared. There was a warning signal I seemed to give off that kept this fish as far away as the pond permitted. Finally, it dawned on my five-year-old mind that the fish had seen me and somehow knew the mission. One day, after sneaking up on him as carefully as I could, I threw my worm into the water. He took the bait and I wound up with a fourteen-inch brook trout. Mystery solved.

For a five-year-old this fish was huge. I ran all the way back home with my prize. I'm sure the size of the fish grew each time the story was told, even with the fish in question sitting on a plate in the refrigerator for anyone to inspect. By the time the day was out it grew to at least two feet and several pounds, depending on who you asked. I didn't care. The point was simple to me and, most likely, to those adults to whom it mattered. Even at five years old I could be trusted to be on my own. I knew where home was, couldn't get lost as long as I stayed within established boundaries, and would always be back for dinner.

Those were the days when the commonwealth of Massachusetts had a defined fishing season. It ended each year on the last day of February and began again on the third Saturday of April (at one time the fifteenth of April). While still beginning on the fifteenth, schools experienced a rate of truancy that could be anticipated, not to mention the number of adults calling in sick to their jobs. Some businesses actually closed on the fifteenth, claiming it was to allow their employees to file taxes. Who were they kidding? The more popular trout streams were elbow to elbow with "sick" employees.

Finally, reason prevailed and the date was changed to the third Saturday, a day off from school and holiday for most workers, taxes having already been filed. Still, there remained tremendous pressure on the streams and usual hot spots for trout.

Eventually came the realization that no benefit for fish was derived from an off-season. Fish of various species spawned at different times. Even different species of trout spawned without regard to the regulations man had placed upon them. The only beneficial thing the otherwise enlightened minds in Boston did was change the "take limit" with the seasons.

The effect was enormous. The early season pressure was relieved and fishing became an enjoyable sport once more. But let's backtrack a bit. It seemed the fifteenth always fell on a school day. Together with the Linder kids who lived across the street, and my sister, Diana, we kids all lived for Opening Day. Diana was the oldest, eleven, and de-facto the one to watch over the rest of us. Ronnie Linder, eight, and his sister, Michelle, six, were both older than me. For at least a week prior to the magical day we prepared, making sure we had worms—plenty of worms. Maybe they would bite like crazy this season. (They never did.)

Kids that were usually hard to get up in the morning to meet the school bus made plans to meet in one kitchen or the other before dawn to get ready for the big event. Our parents thought this was the greatest thing—kids actually getting up early on their own so they could go fishing before they went to school.

The only place we were allowed to fish (for safety reasons) was the little brook up the street. On Opening Day, we seldom caught anything, but the adventure of it all was something not one of us would miss for anything in the world. Opening Day was one of the absolute best days possible in our lives, and we never missed school as a result, though we often went to bed dead tired after returning home in the afternoon.

The truth is on Opening Day the water was usually too high, the temperature too cold, or our skills too unrefined to hook any fish. We really didn't start catching anything until later in the season after things calmed down a bit.

Being the youngest of the bunch, unless I was accompanied by Dad, I was restricted to fishing in the brook while some of the older kids were allowed to fish the various rivers in the area. I respected this restriction, for unbeknownst to the elders it allowed me to hone my skills beyond what might have been expected of a child my age. I came to know every hole and undercut in that little brook and was able to figure out just what the trout hiding there would bite on. Even at this young age I started to return home with my limit almost every time, and often the main course for dinner was trout I had caught that day. These were truly wild trout, totally unaffected by pollution or the questionable food given at any hatchery, and they were delicious.

• • •

The law said trout had to be at least six inches long to be kept; that's a rather small fish. In the spring it seemed every one of them we caught was just under the six-inch limit. The problem was that within minutes of being released, they could all be seen floating belly-up, fatally injured by the hook. In time officials in Boston became aware of the problem as well. Size restrictions were dropped, not that it mattered much. Most of the kids had recognized the situation long before and were keeping any fish that had been hooked too badly to survive. Game wardens stopped issuing citations for under-sized fish. Sometimes leaders have to be led.

Years passed and family events eroded my young optimistic outlook, but the little brook became a place of solace and refuge from events I could not control and had a tremendous impact on my developing person. More times than either of my parents realized I just had to get away with Mitzie, who never left my side, to try and get my thoughts together. I was one very confused child—parents at each other's throats, separated but living within a quarter-mile of each other, an uncle preying on me sexually whenever we were alone and no one believing me when I told them, and nowhere to go. Whenever I brought up what my uncle had done, I was spanked or punished in some other way. Of course he denied all allegations, and who were the adults in my life going to believe?

Whenever I fished the brook, I always started at the tube that came under the road called Route 183. For the first hundred yards or so I was fully visible to my mother working in her hairdressing shop across the street. It was suicide for me to ignore her call if she wanted me to come home for whatever reason, sometimes, I think, just to make sure I was there. I soon learned that if I needed to be alone, really needed to be alone with my thoughts, I had to move farther downstream, and fast. Unless I had reason to believe a lunker was hiding out above the line where she could see me, I rapidly got out of sight and earshot. I had to be alone for a while, with my dog, while I sorted things out. I needed that time to remain sane, or at least pretend to be. In the meantime, I caught fish.

I knew all the good places in that little stream and could almost predict where and how many fish I would catch. On occasion, when my thoughts were particularly deep and troubling, I had to stop off at a favorite hole to catch something to prove where I had been all afternoon. Neither Mom nor Dad ever fully realized what their actions had done to their child, though in later years an understanding seemed to happen, unrelated to their son. They never acknowledged the damage, and life just picked up from where it left off once the acrimony stopped. Through my teens and early adult life my mind debated whether to confront issues that were now on the mend or just let sleeping dogs lie. I chose the latter. They're all gone now. No one will be hurt by what truths come out now.

The brook had surprises in store for me as well. One day, while fishing and undercut, I latched onto a muskrat. Don't ask how or why but Mitzie dispatched the critter before you could say, "Trout." Except for one time I don't think I ever caught a trout more than ten inches long. They just didn't get any bigger than that in such a small stream. Except that once … I caught a seventeen-inch, almost two-pound brook trout in a stream that was hardly two feet wide. I don't know how it got there or escaped previous attempts at capture, but that was one of the best natural fish I have ever caught. No one believed it was caught in the little brook but it was, and no one was more surprised than me.

• • •

Not many people seem to fish this little brook today. What made it easy for us kids back then was the way cattle grazed on both sides. They kept the brush down, making it possible for the angler, a child, to get his bait to float down into the areas where the fish were hiding. Cattle graze on neither side of the brook today and the brush, and weeds have grown in to the point where fishing without entanglement is nearly impossible. I can still see the trout from time to time, still about six to ten inches in length, mostly feeding a Blue Heron or two now. But one of these days I'm going to take a grandchild fishing in what I consider sacred waters. Unless they ever get to read this, they'll never know the full significance of what that little brook has meant to me; it's a great place to learn about life, love—especially love from a dog—and nature untouched. I don't know if I could have survived without the help of Mitzie and that little brook. When I'm gone, I want at least some of my ashes to be scattered there. It's the least I can do in repayment.

Osama and Me

In the late forties and early fifties, if you lived in the rural setting this once was, a shopping trip to town was relatively rare. We grew what we needed, or at least as much of it as we could manage, bought special things when we could, and sometimes went without if it couldn't be raised or purchased easily enough. Raising cows, pigs, turkeys, and an oversize vegetable garden were part of my regular summer activities, especially during my pre-teen years. Everyone pitched in, male or female—we all had duties.

But the chickens ... now they were another matter. There was never a time during this period of my life when we didn't have chickens. They exercised an influence, if not an outright veto, over many daily activities. They had to be fed and watered and the eggs collected, often several times a day. Since I was the youngest, the task of caring for the chickens was mine, the larger animals being adult responsibilities. Frequently this meant not being able to go off with my friends or play baseball when I wanted. More than once I cursed those damn chickens, but in the end, they wound up teaching me more than ever expected.

We didn't just have the obligatory fifty to one hundred chickens all the time, but also at least one rooster. While the hens just go about their business, scratching and pecking around, looking for the next tasty insect or grain, the roosters would strut their stuff, proving to the world they were masters of all they surveyed.

I don't know if I have ever seen an animal display more pride than a rooster. He truly wants you to know he is king. Crowing is not confined to sunrise, though the rooster is certain that the sun would cease to rise if not for his commanding it to do so. Crowing and parading about the yard is the very essence of what it means to be a rooster, demanding you and all other creatures to take note and acknowledge the fact that he is king of, well, everything.

Did you say you wish to challenge his dominion? Be prepared to incur the wrath of the big boy. In every flock, even if there were multiple males, there was always one who emerged as king, the leader of the pack, the khan, and sometimes … the terminator. If one wasn't careful entering the chicken yard, a violent surprise might await the unwary. More than one aggressive bird has drawn blood from me, occasionally even requiring stitches. They can be outright vicious.

I was about six years old when I was forced to reach an understanding with a giant—at least that's how he looked to me—White Leghorn rooster. I caught it from my mother after I dropped the basket of eggs and ran as this mean thing came after me. To this day I don't know whether the swat from Mom hurt worse than any damage that Foghorn-Leghorn would have done, but from that day on I always took a stick while collecting the eggs. He never bothered me when I was feeding or watering, only when collecting eggs.

I never gave this rooster a name, though most of the others that followed were called by something or other. Some later tyrants even responded to their names. But this guy had one much bigger surprise for me; we became friends. It started with a complete cessation of the attacks, followed by his eating right from my hand and even allowing me to pet him. Maybe he finally realized who held the meal ticket. But then it became even more bizarre; he would perch on my shoulder as I walked about the barnyard and crow to his heart's delight. In my child's imagination I was the pirate on the main with a parrot on my shoulder. He never bothered me after we reached our understanding, but others were not so fortunate. Occasionally, he used my shoulder as the launching pad for an attack.

This was the heyday of the county fair, and of course there

was the poultry show. Most of the kids I knew had chickens; it seemed every family had a few. That's just the way things were. One of the categories was a trio: a rooster and two young hens. This was a serious competition between us kids. It was not unusual for a youngster to take a week to select and prepare his trio in the hopes of winning a blue ribbon. And cash.

I had a distinct advantage; my mother was a professional hairdresser, and my chickens, rooster included, got a thorough shampoo, and spent time under the hair dryer. He did not appreciate my efforts at first but then, as he realized how dapper he had become, his pride shone almost as brilliantly as his plumage.

We were not permitted in the exhibition hall during the judging process, but a fair-sized group of kids awaited the results outside. For several minutes loud and occasionally very blue language streamed invectively toward us through the door. Someone was not having a banner day in the judging department. "Just give the son-of-a-bitch the blue ribbon and the hell with it," was the last thing any of us heard distinctly.

As the judges exited the area, one had a blood-soaked handkerchief wrapped around his wrist. Things had not gone his way. When the kids were allowed back in, it was my trio that had the blue ribbon on the cage. White Leghorn was crowing triumphantly, defiantly. He had not allowed anyone to handle his hens. I was tempted to parade him on my shoulder, but I don't think the judge, who was now receiving medical attention for his wounds, would have shown the amount of appreciation my rooster might have commanded.

I don't know what eventually happened to this rooster. I was told a fox got him after he came home. The truth of the matter, I learned later, was that it was risky business putting birds back into your flock after they had been to the show. The threat of infectious disease was too great. I have a hunch Dad took care of these birds after I was in bed that night. In my inadequate way I spent the next several days looking for the fox that did the dastardly deed. I never thought about the chicken and soup we had for dinner the next few days.

Over the years we had different breeds of chicken; both Rhode Island and New Hampshire Reds, Speckled Sussex, Barred Plymouth Rocks, and Buff-Koshen, are only a few I remember, but I know there were others, including several species of bantams. Many of these breeds are hard to find today, except in shows. Most of the chickens commercially grown today are hybrids, "sex-links" as they are called in the trade.

We always had a rooster or two in the flock; I guess fertile eggs were the thing back then. Occasionally, there would be a mean one with an attitude, usually a bantam, but it was some years before I encountered another large bird with the personality of my big White Leghorn. Actually, there were four: King, Prince, Duke, and One-Eyed Jack. Each of these weighed well in excess of fifteen pounds, but they were all as gentle as puppy dogs, and as much beggars. They had free reign about the farm store and greenhouses, never bothering anyone except to beg a bit of donut.

Ah, the donuts. To these extremely handsome roosters, donuts represented the food of the gods. A word to the wise: Do not leave your donut unattended. There are feathered thieves about. All unguarded donuts will be confiscated. More than one customer came to me concerned about a chicken that had stolen his donut.

These roosters were loved by all. They had a fan club that would regularly bring the kids to see them. Jack is memorialized in an oil painting that hangs near the checkout. Sadly, they all met their demise in the jaws of some local dogs.

But then came Osama. In the spring of 2002, I purchased some young pullets, hens just about ready to start their egg-laying careers. Two of this group didn't look quite right. Gender is not as obvious in the world of chickens, at least not at an early age, but these two didn't cluck ... they crowed! What's more, their personalities resembled a hornet more than a hen.

The Prussian wasn't as difficult to deal with since a defect in his stepping caused him to be a little slow, reminiscent of an army goose-step. You at least had warning and could take evasive action. The problem was Osama. He was big, fast, sneaky, and utterly fearless. He also professed equal opportunity hatred. He didn't like anyone, except the hens.

More than once he drew blood from me, usually after a successful attack from behind. He would quickly retreat, dodging any attempt to swat him, and then, after I would leave the pen, he would taunt me with as loud a crow as he was capable of making. Once, after a particularly vicious attack, I caught him by the neck. Mad, bloody revenge in my mind, I threw him against the wall of the chicken coop, expecting to end this nuisance once and for all. But it didn't work. The impact stunned him, but he regained his feet, shook his head as if to clear the cobwebs, and came right back at me as determined as ever.

Part of me was still ready to kill him, but another had a new-found respect for this creature that could stare death in the face and still go forward because it was his job to protect his hens. After finishing the egg collection, I made my retreat from the pen and turned, making eye contact with this fearless creature. He paused for a moment and then let out as loud a crow as he could muster right at my face. He had taken the worst I could dish out and still came back for more, having lost none of his defiance.

I reached an accommodation with Osama shortly thereafter. I would throw food into a corner of the pen before entering. He never ate while I was there collecting the eggs, but as long as the hens were actively picking up grain, he would leave me alone, just watching, carefully positioned between me and his hens.

I never lost any birds while he was alive, but half expected to find a dead coyote or hawk instead. Changing his name occurred to me more than once, but he had become a fixture at the farm, even gaining his own fan club. I had a lot of respect for Osama, the protector of his flock. I have none for the man who would send others to do what he feared to do himself. One has to wonder who was the man and who was the chicken.

I found Osama dead in his pen one morning. He hadn't seemed up to par for a few days, so it wasn't a complete surprise. Despite the scars, I'm going to miss him.

Quest for the Chestnut

One day in 1953 or '54, Al Cooper, my father's best friend at the time, made a spring excursion from New Jersey bearing a gift. It didn't look like much, just a twig wrapped in damp newspaper, but it held the promise of something not seen in the Berkshires for more than forty years: a chestnut tree. This was supposed to be a resistant strain—resistant to the blight that had devastated the entire population of a species and eliminated a way of life.

Where Al got the young seedling I have no idea, but he presented the sprout to my dad with great fanfare. Al had connections with powerful people; once he had been an aid to John D. Rockefeller. This tree was special, a descendant of a tree showing remarkable ability to withstand the fungus infection that had destroyed one of the most important trees in this nation's history. I remember this tiny twig planted with more care than a prize-winning peony, and Dad had several of those he could boast about.

Al assured my father the seedling was not crossbred but rather a descendant of a particular tree showing ability to fend off the blight. Dad didn't trust man-made hybrids, only those that occurred naturally. For at least a couple weeks the two men held their breaths until leaves began to sprout. The little tree would make it, but this was only the beginning of the quest, the struggle for the very survival of the species.

The American chestnut is unique; especially suited to growing in the eastern U.S. and upper reaches of the Mid-West, it rarely if ever failed to produce a crop. The nut is smaller in size than its European or Asian cousins, but over centuries it fed large populations of both Native Americans and pioneers, not to mention massive numbers of wildlife. While other wild nut trees tend to blossom early and are sometimes killed by a late frost, the chestnut seldom flowers before June, giving it a sort of insurance policy against late cold weather. When all else failed, one could count on chestnuts as a survival food. All you had to do was gather them in the fall. Settlers quickly learned the value of this tree from the Native Americans. They also discovered the unique rot-resistant quality of the wood. To this day, one may still find hand-hewn timbers in old buildings and barns.

One might be tempted to say the pioneers were partially responsible for the decline of the chestnut, but that would be a false assumption; when cut to the ground, the chestnut had the ability to sprout again from its own roots. When the blight was first noticed, most of the Northeast was working off second and even third growth chestnut wood. The chestnut is remarkably resilient.

Few photos of mature old growth chestnuts survive, but there is good reason why they were referred to as "Redwoods of the East;" their size was stupendous. Often in excess of two hundred feet in height and more than ten feet in trunk diameter, groves of chestnuts dominated the landscape, especially in the western parts of the Carolinas. In North Carolina, one tree was more than seventeen feet thick at the base. After frost in autumn the nuts, which are about the size of a quarter coin, would fall like rain—or more appropriately like hail—reportedly covering the ground as much as waist-deep! There was always more than enough for people and wildlife, rural families earning extra cash by sending sacks to the cities, especially New York. Largely gone now are the street vendors selling bags of freshly roasted nuts on the corners.

Dad told me he fondly remembered a massive chestnut growing across the street from the church he attended as a child. One particular year left a deep impression. There had been a hard frost, but after Sunday services the sun had come out and warmed the air to just the right temperature. While children danced and cheered encouragement, a giant of a man thumped the base of the tree with a railroad tie. The nuts fell so heavily people caught them with their clothes. Our family brought home bushels for the winter, and this was an annual event.

The fungus disease that brought these behemoths to the brink of extinction is thought to have come from Asia with some Chinese cousins of our domestic chestnut. The Chinese version demonstrates a complete tolerance of the disease, which first shows itself as an orange-colored lesion that eventually works deeper into the bark until it cuts off all sap circulation.

When first noticed in Brooklyn's famous Prospect Park around the turn of the century, foresters at first attempted to remove affected limbs, then whole trees but to no avail. The blight spores were airborne. Within a few seasons the entire Northeast was infected. Nothing could stop the spread. Even the giants of North Carolina were brought to the ground.

Groves showed varying degrees of resistance. Enterprising breeders attempted to cross the most promising of these with tolerant Asian strains in order to save the species. Some modicum of success was attained but this was still not the true American chestnut, often being more than one quarter Asian and still succumbing to the blight, albeit at a later age than their purebred counterparts.

$$\bullet \quad \bullet \quad \bullet$$

Many years have passed since Al and my father planted the little sprout. The two best friends are both gone now. I remember them saying no one ever plants a tree for himself; you plant it for a future generation. The tree they planted grew quickly, up to about twenty feet, and had numerous burrs and nuts, but I was never able to gather any. The squirrels, or deer, or whatever critter, always got them first.

Then I noticed the telltale orange scars. I tried using fungicides but was unable to alter the tree's fate. Branch after branch withered in just one season, but it sprang back again from the roots the next spring. Surely there was hope. This spontaneous re-generation took place many times over the years and I believe is still going on. The fungus seems to only affect what is above ground. Although this particular tree is doomed, I discovered an offspring about fifty feet away, something probably planted by a squirrel, and this one shows remarkable vigor. It grew straight and spreading, and with a meticulous inspection done at least once a year, I could find no sign of the disease. Three years ago, it bore its first nuts, but the wildlife got them all again. Last year in 2019 it had very few and I was able to retrieve some, but for an unexplained reason they disappeared. I think my wife unknowingly threw them out, but who's to say?

Two medium-sized pines tended to shade my juvenile chestnut, so I decided to remove them to help the little tree along. Last autumn, with the wind blowing lightly and from a desirable direction, I started my chainsaw. What I had not counted on was a grape vine that bound the two pines together above the chestnut. As one pine came down the vine swung it around and it fell directly on my little tree, giving it an unmerciful slashing. I was heartbroken. One main limb was still intact, but the bulk of the little tree was in splinters. I tried to splice it together, but it appeared too far gone. But then I remembered chestnut trees are remarkably resilient; maybe it would re-sprout in the spring.

Several times during the winter I went out to visit that tree, hoping against hope it would come back at least a little. I think I felt more guilt over a tree than I have felt over almost any other misdeed in my life. That little tree had depended on me and I had let it down by my carelessness.

Whenever a species is threatened the survivors grow stronger, and as these individuals eventually succumb, they leave behind new generations, each with a little more resistance to whatever it is that did the parents in. Witness the once majestic elms; this constant re-generation is starting to bear fruit. With humans we hope the young will be just a bit smarter. This does not always pan out, but we can hope.

In the case of my little chestnut, it was already taller than its parent had ever grown, and it had borne fruit on several occasions rather than the usual one or two times common with its late ancestors. Vigor! This tree had grown between four and six feet per season. I could have cried over what happened to it.

Spring came at last and although many plants and trees had already come alive, my little chestnut was still dormant, but that was normal. They are always late; it is part of their survival strategy. At last, near the end of May, it stirred and suddenly burst forth as if nothing out of the ordinary had occurred. Where branches had broken off new sprouts appeared, so many I would have to trim out the weaker ones to allow the tree to re-shape itself. And on the one remaining good limb there were burrs, perhaps not as many as I would like to see, but that the tree is saying, "I'm still here. It's going to take more than an errant pine to bring me down." And still there is absolutely no sign of the disease, though its thoroughly infested parent is growing only fifty feet away.

I'm watching those burrs like a hawk. Squirrels beware! Stay tuned. Perhaps redemption is at hand.

As of 2020, not only has the tree survived, it is producing nuts on the new branches. Unfortunately, the deer and the squirrels have won again and I couldn't collect any nuts, but there is another chestnut a distance away from the original that is showing the same vigor.

*Life Lessons
& Anecdotes*

Not on an Empty Stomach

Times were hard during the Great Depression. The unemployment rate was officially pegged somewhere around thirty percent. Most said it was closer to fifty. There was no security net. If you were out of a job, finding work was almost impossible. With no work there was no money, with no money, no place to live and frequently... no food.

Whether you lived in the city or the country, the story was the same. It might have been easier outside the city because you at least had an opportunity to raise something, to hunt, or to fish. (Dad once told me that until '32 when he got a job, there was no meat on the table unless he shot it. Game wardens tended to ignore desperate people only trying to feed their families.) Most cities had some social service agency to help feed desperate people, but for how long? In the rural areas, possibilities existed, but charity organizations had fewer resources. Quickly overrun by the needy, often those migrating out of cities, soup kitchens became unable to help those in need. Deserving and frantic families sometimes had to be turned away, individuals refused as a matter of routine, a person alone judged to be able to handle life's problems better than a family with children.

Those who had a job did whatever necessary to keep it and scrape by on whatever they made, often a pittance. A few dollars a week, a garden, chickens, maybe a pig and a cow... a little luck... and a family could get by. Barely. Repairing things, making do, getting by, one day to the next, one month was the most one could hope for.

My father was one of the lucky ones. He had a job maintaining looms in a textile mill, even if it was only a few days a week. How he got it and managed to keep it is still the topic of conversations and one of the reasons the name "Taft" came about, but that's a story for another time.

Many called Dad a squirrel or packrat, and with good reason. He never threw anything out. If he could think of any conceivable use for something, it was saved. Criticism came from many sides, mostly from those more fortunate, but Dad not only survived the Great Depression, he thrived after a fashion because he seldom had to buy anything. He opened Steve's Fix-It Shop with the motto "You break it and I'll fix it – no matter what it is." He had spare parts for almost anything and never lost a challenge.

It was summer 1933, and the "livin' ain't easy." The market went up a little, then dropped like a rock. Main Street followed along. Businesses and banks failed one after another, but the little shop out on Division Street kept humming away repairing life's essentials, often in exchange for a chicken or a promise. But that day was a Sunday; chores were done, the lawn had been mowed. It was almost time to take it easy, but there was still the hedge to be trimmed.

Dad started on the edge near the driveway, the part that could make it difficult to see when pulling out with the car, the car that didn't exist, into the traffic that was never a hazard. He failed to see the man approach. It was as if he materialized out of the bushes or the fields... but Steve heard his voice.

"I'll trim those hedges if you'll give me something to eat."

Startled, Dad engaged the man in conversation while he looked him over. Down on luck, not all were friendly; some would kill for a quarter. Little more than rags threatened to fall off the man's toothpick frame, but he had a friendly attitude and bearing. The two could have been best friends in another life, but here fate found them, one anticipating Sunday dinner and the other having trouble remembering the last time he had eaten anything.

Dad's sister, my aunt Tessie, was preparing the meal. They lived in the family home by themselves, the rest of the family deceased or moved away. She observed the encounter from the kitchen and after deciding the young man posed no threat told her brother to invite him in. They could use company; there was extra. No one should go hungry, not in their home.

We'll call this fellow Ed; I don't believe I was ever told his name. He seemed intelligent, though reserved. It was obvious that if not for hunger he was a man of few words, but he had trouble even making the slightest of smiles, so deep was his despair.

After dinner they sat and visited, commiserating on the country's state of affairs. Ed was from New York City, the Bronx to be exact. He had walked to Great Barrington (he had no money for the train) because a friend had told him there was an opportunity in a paper mill. The friend's brother knew someone in management. But the job was taken by the time Ed arrived. He tried all the many small sawmills, every business, any angle he could think of but there was nothing, and he had nothing left. All his possessions were gone, either sold to survive or re-possessed.

In the city he had been a loan officer at a bank, one that failed. In the summer of 1929, he had become engaged to the daughter of one of the bank's vice presidents, on his way up the ladder, showing drive and enthusiasm, a go-getter, a major promotion on the way. He bought a new car, a Packard, lived in a good neighborhood, and was seen at the right social events. In general, he enjoyed the good life. It all came crashing down before Christmas. His fiancé had a complete breakdown after her father committed suicide. Soon, she followed her father. Everything in life seemed to evaporate. In a matter of months, he was homeless and broke. He'd stood in lines for hours to find the soup had run out a few men before him. "There might be more... tomorrow."

Ed had last eaten three days ago, but the volunteers warned they were getting short and would have to restrict efforts to families only. "No one had been outright abusive," he explained,

"There was just nothing they could do. Steve and Tessie were the first who helped."

Before he left, Ed asked for a pad of paper and pencil. There were letters he wanted to write thanking friends. Dad found clothes he no longer needed, thinking it might improve Ed's appearance. He loaned Ed the use of his razor. Maybe his luck would change if he looked presentable.

Ed still wanted to trim the hedge, but Dad insisted the good company was more than enough payment. They wished each other well, shook hands and Ed was on his way. "To Lenox," he said. "Lots of wealthy people have homes up there, maybe I can find a job caretaking."

Two days passed. On Tuesday, a day off from the mill, Dad was fixing someone's washing machine out in his work-shed—transmission problems—when the police arrived. Not just the local chief, Dan MacCarty, a good friend, but also a state trooper, and they came in separate cars. It was obvious they weren't just stopping by to see where the fish were biting. They got right to the point.

"Do you recognize this man?" the trooper asked as he handed Dad a photograph.

The eyes of the man in the picture were closed, as if asleep, and his head was cocked at a strange angle. Dad knew in an instant that the picture was Ed, and he said so.

They asked more questions, which Dad answered, the whole time wondering what they were getting at.

Finally, the trooper handed Dad a piece of paper. Dad recognized it as having come from the pad of stationery they had given Ed. The writing was neat and orderly to the extreme, precise, and addressed to Steve and Tessie, Division Street, Great Barrington. Dan MacCarty explained they were the only two by those names on Division Street.

The letter thanked them for all they had done and asked forgiveness for what he was about to do. They were the kindest people he had met in years. Steve and Tessie were genuine; unlike the shallow money hunters he had known all his life. He had given up on any future and resigned himself to one last request, and Steve and Tessie had granted it. They had provided him with one of the best meals he'd had in a long time and now he could end the misery. He did not want to die on an empty stomach.

"Your friend hung himself in a barn in Lenox," the trooper said.

Dan MacCarty later recounted how Dad turned white as a sheet. Tessie vomited violently when she heard the news. Though frequently asked, it was more than a year before they invited another stranger in for a meal.

Burma Christmas, 1941

Joe Sadlowski was a volunteer. They were all volunteers. None had raised his hand. Not necessary. The whole unit of U.S. Army Engineers was volunteered by someone higher up, maybe as high up as Roosevelt. They never knew just why their unit was to be sent overseas, only that the order came and they had to go to Burma to build a road for supplies to make the journey to General Chennault's Flying Tigers in China. Officially the Tigers were the only volunteers. Neither Joe nor anyone ever asked how or why. You didn't do that in this man's army, you just did what you were told, and the dogs of coming war were barking.

The heat was bad, bugs even worse. Malaria, dysentery, beriberi, fevers too numerous to count—take your pick of diseases. Any in sequence or combination became constant companions. Men found themselves seeking duties close to the latrine to avoid painful and embarrassing accidents. After a while, even that didn't matter. By far malaria was the worst. They quickly learned if you came down with malaria you had better hope someone was nearby to take care. The intense fever was what killed you, not the little parasite. Joe told me everyone was so weak the medics invented a new diagnosis: AOE, Accumulation of Everything.

Robust and healthy when they arrived, few weighed more than a hundred pounds by the advent of the rainy season. That's when things got worse. Mosquitoes multiplied exponentially, so many that few men paid attention to the constant feeding frenzy. The only question was how much blood you had left to give.

Still, since they were not far from the coast, supplies arrived on a regular basis using their road. The bulldozers had their diesel, the men had their Army food, and the march continued, making even better progress than anticipated. Gaining higher ground, the air cooled, mosquitoes became less active, disease lightened its grip, and general health and attitude improved. Some even gained back a few pounds. But the farther up and into the mountains they progressed, the longer the supply-line. Soon, necessities became more memory than reality. Creature comforts— food and medicine, even fuel for the bulldozers— could no longer be taken for granted. Periodically, the Japanese army cut the road behind them.

A hastily constructed airfield was supposed to help, but as with any solution, a problem arose. The Japanese Air corps took exception to supply planes trying to make it "over the Hump," enough exception that few were fortunate enough to complete the trip, and those that did often contained precious little cargo. Forward progress slowed to a crawl.

Now a C-46 aircraft could technically carry almost twenty thousand pounds. The problem was that the same C-46 couldn't fly higher than twenty thousand feet, and that was with an empty cargo. The lowest passes were at nearly sixteen thousand. As had been demonstrated before, prior planning was not the military's strongest suit. The Zeros did not need to intercept the supply planes; mountains did it for them. It was not until later, when surviving pilots told their stories, that the brass finally understood they had to have more horsepower to clear the Himalayas. Converted B-24s finally did the job.

It was 1941. We were not officially at war until Pearl Harbor. Hitler was raising hell in Europe, Mussolini in Africa, Stalin was nobody's friend, and Tojo was taking over Eastern Asia. The U.S. was not actually fighting except for the volunteers in China, Burma, and England. The man I still call Uncle Joe out of respect, even though he is technically a second cousin (my mother's first cousin) was one of these volunteers, along with a group of his friends from Housatonic, a close-knit community in western Massachusetts. In those days if a group of friends or relatives joined, they could serve together.

"Do you know how hungry you have to be to feel like you have to vomit all the time, but you can't because there's nothing there? You want to go to the latrine but there's nothing. And you have to keep working because you have a job and you still have to dodge the occasional bullet coming from the jungle."

Some of the natives helped; you just didn't know who to trust. Was the food they gave you safe, were they spying?

You ate bugs for protein, grass and leaves for fiber, and whatever game happened to cross your path... even rats. "Rats aren't bad, as long as you skin and gut them properly. Some were really big, as big as small deer and as mean as a hornet, but they made a pretty good soup," Joe said.

On Christmas Eve, times were desperate; everyone was hungry and weak, morale too low to measure. No one wanted to be there, especially that night. Men were crying openly. Thoughts of home and Christmases past emphasized the predicament. A lone C-46 limped into the strip, the first in a week, obvious damage to its tail section. Chances were it would not fly for a while, if ever again.

Eager GI's braved the dust storm as the miracle from the sky taxied to a halt. It had been too long since the last landing. It might be a month before the next. But this was Christmas Eve... and miracles happen, even there.

Drums of much-needed fuel, K-rations, C-rations, even those God-awful dried potatoes, quinine tablets and other medicine, mail, and a package for one Joseph Sadlowski from his cousin Helen, my mother, were off-loaded into excited hands.

All the provisions were more than welcome, but a surprise waited in the mysterious package. Joe opened it carefully, as if trying to prevent damage to delicate contents. (Only later did he even think about what kind of handling it had to have endured to get there.) He said there were at least fifty faces jockeying for position to see the goodies.

It contained mostly what had been expected and hoped for:

nearly melted chocolate bars (the sweet kind, not the bitter Army stuff), toothpaste, razor blades, a jar of homemade jam, a few personal things, and a giant loaf of homemade bread. The bread was as hard as a concrete block and about as heavy, but beggars could not be choosers. It had to have been baked at least a month ago.

A bayonet served as a bread knife but the thing did not want to be cut. The blade only went so far before meeting full resistance. Finagling revealed that the loaf of bread contained a huge bottle of homemade blackberry brandy, baked right into it both to avoid the censors and to provide shock-resistance in travel.

Now, a package of this kind was not something a man would even think of keeping for himself, even under better conditions. Sharing was how one stayed alive, and Joe shared everything with his "brothers," especially the brandy.

It's not hard to imagine how men on the verge of starvation could feel better with just a small amount of alcohol and a little strawberry jam on stale bread. They all agreed knowing that someone at home was thinking of them meant more than anything else. I have personally met and talked with four of the men who were there that night and they all say that was the absolute best Christmas anyone could hope for. Starving men hugged one another and sang Christmas carols for hours. No one moaned or groaned about where they were or what they were doing. They gave thanks for good fortune and fellowship, back-slapping and joke-telling, laughing into the night. And no one died. Death and misery just weren't allowed.

The thought of the odds that small package had to overcome to make its way to Joe and arrive on that most meaningful day are staggering, a miracle by any standard. It took more than week before the next plane made it in, a month before the road was re-opened.

• • •

A few years ago, I was at Midnight Mass with my family. Uncle Joe was nearby with his family. When the congregation sang "Silent Night," Joe broke down in tears and I, along with several who knew, helped him from church. He had learned that one of his buddies from that night so many years ago had passed away. Bill had been sick, but his friends had been hoping against the odds. "Silent Night" was too much for Uncle Joe, and time was using up these men's miracles.

Joe reunited with Bill and his passed buddies two Christmases later. When they come together, I hope the bread will not be as stale, but I'll bet the brandy will taste as sweet. I'm sure the carols will be sung with gusto and passion, dog tags jingling with every toast. Each Christmas Eve more brothers will arrive at the party till they're all there. My mother will personally deliver a fresh supply of bread, homemade jam, and more brandy. Likely the pilot of the Zero who shot up the tail of that C-46 will show up and be just as welcome as the guys who were shooting from the jungle. Together they'll all raise a toast, as one. Because miracles and brotherhood happen at Christmas.

Even in the jungles of a war-torn Burma, the baby Jesus can smile.

Last Wishes

Fate has plans for each of us. Will any one of us live up to expectations, our own or those of others? Will we even get the chance? Or will our hopes be thrown out the window and fall like fertile seeds on the pavement rather than the garden? I never met the young man of this story, but I've seen his picture on his mother's mantle and thumbed through a much-read dog-eared album of his accomplishments. Joan is still devastated over his loss, even though it has been forty years or more. She still cries over what might have been but can take solace in one major accomplishment on his behalf: she was able to keep her promise.

Justin was always a gifted athlete; you know, the guy that was always picked first. He deserved to be. He was damned good at anything athletic. Quarterback of football teams from Pee Wee through high school and seemingly always on the winning team, star shooting guard on the basketball team and claiming the championship in every division he played. Justin ran a sub-ten-second hundred-yard dash and was in the high school state golf finals shooting sub-par rounds as often as not. But it was baseball where he really shined.

Not many batters in high school can hit a fastball going over ninety miles per hour. Couple that with a twelve-six curveball in the mid-seventies and a couple of un-named pitches that defy reality and you are unbeatable. He once had twenty strikeouts in a seven-inning game.

Everyone wanted him, college and pro. He chose college, going to the University of Massachusetts Amherst, and in his freshman year he took UMass to the brink of the College World Series. Expectations were high in Amherst. Next year couldn't come fast enough, but first there was the rest of the summer.

Rather than play in a semi-pro league, Justin opted to sign on with a group of assorted collegians taking the American sport of baseball to Eastern Europe and the Soviet Union. The now nineteen-year-old and high draft pick of the Red Sox was dazzling, not allowing an earned run for the entire trip. The scouts were salivating, but then… the Achilles heel.

Justin was a body builder and had the body to prove it. Often he drank a quart of milk rather than water, scarfed down raw eggs rather than cooked, and ate most of his food raw or only lightly cooked. He continued his eating habits throughout the European tour, thoroughly surprising teammates and hosts.

Then the other shoe dropped. The teams were playing in the Ukraine when the disaster at Chernobyl occurred. The real problem was they were not told until more than two weeks after the fire. The tour was cut short and players sent back to the States. Within a month of return Justin seemed to lose vim and vigor. He could no longer work out, the fastball was not there, and his bones ached to the point he had trouble getting out of bed in the morning. He was diagnosed with an incurable, highly aggressive form of bone cancer. He never returned to Amherst.

Everyone knew Justin had what it took to make it to the big-time. The Red Sox even flew in the best doctors they could find, anywhere, but to no avail. Within three months he was gone.

It's easy to blame Justin's death on what happened at Chernobyl, and it might be the correct diagnosis, but his life is only a part of the story, albeit a tragic part. He most likely would have pitched in the major leagues; everyone I have talked to, including so-called experts, agreed. Justin had talent and ability in spades with room to spare. At Pittsfield High School he is still regarded as a legend. At UMass he is held on the same level as Doctor J. who also played for only one season but left a mark yet unequaled.

Justin's last wish, as he lay on his deathbed, was to be cremated and his ashes scattered in a major league ballpark. The logical choice was of course the Red Sox since they had drafted him, but there were strictly enforced regulations against such things at Fenway Park. Try as they might none of the family was able to buck the bureaucracy. Entreaties at other venues met with a similar fate. Justin's ashes remained on the mantelpiece, causing tears from time to time.

Years passed, divorce, a move South for a new beginning in St. Petersburg, and Justin's ashes wound up on a different mantelpiece but still with his mother. Too much furniture arrived for a house that was way too small. Something must go…

Joan placed an ad in the *Times*. Maybe someone was looking for a dining room set. Lo and behold, someone was looking, and that someone was my brother, Stan, a former colleague of Joan's and a former math teacher of Justin from Pittsfield High.

Stan had already been living in St. Petersburg for a few years and put down new roots. Joan was a new arrival, and a longtime friendship renewed. Casual evenings, a night out here and there but no serious relationship ever developed. They were good friends, and friends help one another.

The City of St. Petersburg had just built Tropicana Field in the hope of luring a major league team, possibly the Dodgers, but alas, it didn't happen. The fully enclosed stadium sat idle while the American League debated where their newest expansion should take place.

Stan knew prominent people, some of whom were connected with the city and the stadium, which began to look more like a five hundred-million-dollar white elephant all the time. Despite his connections, when he tried to fulfill Justin's last wish of having his ashes spread on a field, the answer came back: Sorry, but it's league policy, even though they didn't have a team yet. The answer was always the same no matter how many times Stan called or who he talked to. But then it happened. On his last call he talked to an individual who had news not yet out in the public domain: the American League had awarded St. Petersburg a franchise.

Maybe this man was so elated, maybe he felt sorry for the

guy who kept calling asking to do the same impossible thing, or maybe he was just plain tired of just having to say no all the time. Stan was put on hold while something went on in the background, but when the man came back on the line Stan was transferred to the groundskeeper's office.

"No, it's definitely against all rules and I can't be a party to anything that could jeopardize the reputation of the organization, but we wouldn't be against your bringing the ashes here for a visit. You see, we're still not officially a major league park... No, no we're closed but it's not widely known we leave Gate C unlocked in case of emergency, fire, or whatever. The switch for the emergency lights is just inside the gate on your left. Make sure you turn them off when you leave. Oh, and don't come before ten. Security will still be here. And be gone by midnight. The official announcement will be made at that time."

At approximately 10:30 that night, Joan and Stan with Justin's remains entered Tropicana Field through Gate C. The light switch was on the left and the field gate door was open. When Joan and Stan left almost an hour later, the pitcher's mound was just a little taller. At 12:01 it was announced St. Petersburg was going to have its major league team.

They did remember to turn off the lights.

Shoot the Patriot

Though I never served in the military, I still consider myself patriotic. If I saw a real threat and had some means, any means, to deter, deflect, or defeat it I would be first in line, at this age probably only to take a bullet aimed at another. But back during the height of the war in Vietnam, I saw friends drafted, cajoled into "volunteering," and otherwise swept up into the morass our leaders said was the only way to stop the dominoes from falling. Nothing could have been further from the truth. In hindsight, this war had a lot less to do with the spread of communism than with the making of uncountable sums of money. On further analysis, that statement is probably true of most wars, but this one we could easily call, "The Wall Street War."

In my younger years, I was like most Americans—my country could do no wrong. The election of JFK—a man whom I had the pleasure of meeting, conversing and shaking hands with at one time—left a sense of euphoria, an aura about my thoughts concerning the good ole USA. If one wanted to think about a "generation gap," this guy was one of us not one of them, and I was with him.

Unlike a great many of my classmates in prep school who were mostly interested in the latest from "Eight Mile Road," I was into politics and, some might call it, leadership. Whether he was right or wrong, Jack Kennedy was a leader, and I would have followed him into hell. While virtually all my classmates were listening to The Beach Boys, The Four Seasons, or any number of the fine sixties' groups, I was following The Cuban Missile

Crisis. Not on the Top Forty List of many radio stations.

How many of my classmates or others at that school, just outside Detroit, realized the severity of the situation, I don't know, but some did, I assume. I was glued to the live broadcast from the U.N. when ambassador Adlai Stevenson called the Russian ambassador, Dobrynin, on the carpet, telling him, "We're going to stay here till hell freezes over until you tell us whether you have missiles in Cuba."

The determination shown by one of the best diplomats this country has ever produced was just too much for me. Much to the chagrin of my roommate, who was like-minded, I burst onto the corridor of our dormitory announcing, "We got them now!"

Doors up and down the corridor opened with surprised faces wondering just what the hell was going on. The din of rock and roll was all one could hear, but our proctor, a Catholic priest, also stepped into the corridor, pointed at me, and gave me a big thumbs up. He had been listening and knew where I was coming from.

By the way, there was a town in Michigan not far from our school called Hell, and the postmaster of Hell, Michigan sent a letter to Mr. Stevenson explaining that it occurred a little later that year, but Hell Creek froze over just before the New Year. Mr. Stevenson sent a humorous reply asking him to send pictures. Fortunately, the crisis seemed over by then.

If there was one moment in time where I can say I came of age that was it. Virtually all these young men were either of military age or approaching it and had no idea what they were in for. We were less than thirty miles from Detroit, surrounded by what had to be considered prime targets, and they could not have cared less about what was going on in the world. The latest sound from The Shirrells meant more than what their leaders were doing to save their asses from a nuclear holocaust.

After graduation and summer break, I was off to Boston College. The Cuban Missile Crisis was over; we won, right? It's back to the same old optimism. I played freshman football, ran fall track and pursued studies in the School of Education, probably in that order of importance. I just missed the Dean's List in my first semester, but I'd do better next time.

Then JFK was killed in Dallas. The whole world fell apart.

Everyone on high was lying to us. I vacillated between, "I don't know where" and "Just what the hell is going on?" Nothing meant anything anymore. I considered drugs, readily available, especially LSD, but didn't succumb. I trusted that I would be able to think this thing through.

Time passed, things got worse in Vietnam, the hard edge on my soul mellowed a bit but the war on the other side of the world refused to go away and instead got worse by the day.

Let's play this thing out. Martha and I got married in July, just after we both graduated. I had a student deferment from the draft, but all bets were off now that I was out of school. I had a job as a teacher in the Pittsfield Public Schools, but they offered no consideration in calling for deferments. I was just as eligible as the next guy. 1A.

I was not called, and I still can't figure out why. Everyone I know who was eligible was drafted. The following June, Martha gave birth to Christine. I am now 1Y and not so high on the list. If the draft board had called, I would have gone but the lottery came up. I am number 305, "highly unlikely." Shortly after Christine's birth I learned of the deaths of two close friends from college. John Coll was cut in half by a machine gun burst and Louis Favuzza took one from a sniper. I knew both these fine young men up close and personal. If they went into harm's way, it was because it was the right thing to do. At least that was what their government insisted.

My best friend all through college, Ken Hogan, rotated through the system three times, never for more than a couple months at a time, wounded all three times, but somehow survived both mentally and physically. His wife says he wakes up screaming now and then, but he is an accountant today. He has been called to testify in major-league cases, but no mere lawyer can intimidate Ken Hogan. He has stared death in the face and defeated it. Two high-profile cases, including the AIG mess in

New York, have proven that already. No untested lawyer stands a chance against this proven warrior. Ken's eyes will make mincemeat of him.

• • •

Hank and I hit it off from the beginning. We both came from working class families, got through college, married and found decent teaching jobs. We were natural companions if not dear friends. Sometimes he came to my place and we shot the shit about anything going on, especially the Vietnam War. We both had similar views; something was wrong, what we didn't know, but we could speculate. It made for good conversation. A couple of beers, some backslapping, and we had all the world's problems solved.

Sometimes, not very often but occasionally, it happened at Hank's house where we shared our takes on world events with his father. Hank's mother was deceased, I knew not when, but his father, a gregarious, white-haired, almost patrician sort of mentor as much as parent freely joined in the conversation. Now retired, he might have been lonely, but he had a lifetime of experience to share. He often spoke of life in Austria.

I had to like this guy. He could have been anyone's father, the guiding light, but he knew how to have a little fun when the time was right. He could give fatherly advice, admonish bad behavior, give praise when deserved; he was perfect. More than once, I felt he was holding back.

One day, Hank and I met for a beer after work, not something unusual. A friend joined us, have another. A gal we both knew from years ago... have another. Pretty soon it was later than either of us realized. He had to get home to Dad, and me to Martha.

We both went together; I must have been less drunk because he let me drive, leaving his car in the parking lot. Another buddy would help him retrieve it tomorrow, or the next day. When we got to Hank's place it became obvious that all of us, including

Hank's father, were on a similar schedule of consumption. Hank's wife at the time was a nurse, working a late shift. The old man was maybe one or two up on us but still lucid enough to carry on a conversation. I'm glad we got there safely and refused one for the road. If anything, I might need time before I attempted to make it the rest of the way, but the old man was in good form.

Hank and I had been discussing the merits of the war both before our journey home and now with his somewhat inebriated father; not to say we were in much better shape than the old man. Our conversation had revolved around whether it was more patriotic to serve in a war we both felt was wrong or to move to Canada or some other place where the Selective Service could not force us to fight to just keep fighting. We both shared the idea that our children would be fighting; we could see no end.

The old man settled the argument in a way that changed both our lives, Hank's probably more than mine. "Shut up and sit down," he said with more force than I had ever heard from him and making no attempt to conceal a heavy accent, he held court. The only discernable difference was the authoritarian take on his message. We were to listen, no questions. He had listened while we had semi-drunkenly farbled on about the War and just who could call himself a patriot.

"You speak of patriotism. I know of this, more than you will ever know. When my country called, I was there, maybe first in line, but I had to fight to be there; so many others wanted to be ahead of me. I believed what they said—the Jews were evil, the Aryan race was supreme, no one could stop us, destiny was on our side. It was our *patriotic* duty to make destiny happen. It was all in our hands. The world was in our hands.

"I believed that. I really did. So did everyone else. The message felt intoxicating after what we had been through, the Weimar Republic and all. You couldn't even buy a loaf of bread with a wheelbarrow load of marks. Gold was the only thing of value and only the rich had any." He paused as he took another pull on his beer. "And they had it all.

"From the cloud of dust emerged a voice, one we had been searching for, a voice saying we had done nothing wrong, but the world owed us. We should demand payment. And we followed his lead." He emptied his bottle.

"Do you think I got up every morning thinking this was the day I would do as much evil on the world as I was capable?" He spoke directly to his son. "I was SS in the German Army. I rose through the ranks to become Captain, a leader. I only saw Austria as a visitor, an occupier, but I knew enough about it to pass as Austrian, but I can tell you about Bremen and Auschwitz and Stettin where I grew up.

"Our family was poor. Of course, everyone was poor except for the wealthy, and they were very rich. They had guards so it was hard to get anything from them, but I learned how to steal things so we could stay alive. We poor wound up stealing from one another when times were really bad. I won't tell you how bad they were; you wouldn't believe. Some of us were going to starve. My job was to make sure it wasn't anyone from our family. There were five of us children, and our father had been killed in the first war. I was the oldest. I did what I could to provide for our mother and the others. My only sister, Gertrude—Trude, we called her—died of typhus. No one could afford the cost of a hospital or doctor. The doctors, mostly Jews, demanded payment up front before they would even see a patient. If you couldn't pay you were on your own, and sometimes you died. Trude died." He looked away for a moment as if reflecting on what he might have done differently.

"Hungry. We were hungry all the time. As soon as they became old enough my brothers worked at helping the family out. I had no life, neither did they. Every waking moment was consumed with keeping hunger at bay. I was lucky to have two meals a day, no matter what it was. I, we, all ate things dogs wouldn't eat. Often, we ate dogs, cats, rats, any animal we could catch; a chicken was a prize, but you had to be careful when you stole one of those." He gave a hint of a smile. "I think I still have scars on my ass from a shotgun load of rock salt I got one night, but I got the chicken. It was painful but Mama got most of the salt out while the soup cooked on the stove. You did what you had to do. I'm not proud. I just wanted to live and not be hungry. I was always hungry before my twentieth birthday. Always.

"Then came the savior. I heard this voice telling me we were not guilty. We had done nothing wrong. We had to believe in ourselves and the destiny of the Fatherland to claim our rightful place in the world. When he said the Jews were behind all the misery we had endured, I believed him because I had witnessed first-hand. What had happened to my sister as a result of a Jewish doctor who would not help her. It never dawned on me that not all doctors were Jewish but no doctor, Jewish or not, would have helped us without payment.

"I was in the palm of his hand. He told it like I had seen it. I was not the only one. Millions of others heard his message and it rang true. It may not have been completely true but there was enough in it to make anyone believe, at least for a while. When I look at what is going on in the Middle East and many other places in the world, I see the seeds of another disaster, far worse than the one I fought. Weaponry has advanced many times over; mankind has not. The uber-wealthy will never have all they want, and the poor will always be chasing an ear of corn hung out in front of them, just like the mule. Humans are not stupid, just vulnerable, and the worst part is they want to believe. We all believe what we want to believe, what we want to be true. Slick politicians play on our emotions all the time."

I saluted the old man, though Hank was clearly uncomfortable. This was truly a philosopher of unrealized insight, but he was revealing family secrets with potentially devastating consequences. Hank was ready to throttle the old man just to shut him up, but this had been building far too long. There was no holding him back.

I tried to give my friend assurances that whatever was said in this room would not leave it, but his anxiety only increased. He opened another beer and handed me one as well. Perhaps he wanted me to get drunk enough to not remember anything, but

I wasn't there yet, and I was in the presence of a prophet. The old man was telling us what I'm sure others had been thinking but no one had the guts to come out with. He was old enough he felt he had nothing left to lose, but maybe he could prevent someone from making the same mistakes.

"My mother, perhaps a little wiser from age and experience, cautioned me against diving in too deep, but even she listened to every speech on the old radio we had in the apartment. The man who lived there before was, I think, killed in the first war. The radio was there when we moved in, broken, but a friend fixed it. It became the only way we were able to have contact with anything outside our little world.

"That radio. Our link to reality. We heard about everything. After our foraging trips, my brothers were now old enough to join me; we listened to 'der Fuhrer,' to wonderful music. I remember Mama dancing across the floor to Strauss, sock mending still in her hand, but in her mind she was in the finest ballroom in Berlin with her prince, now just a photo in his army uniform on the shelf, an artifact of what we once had known. I was a small child when he left for the war. We heard he had been killed but we were never able to bury a body. She might have still been hoping.

"But mostly we listened to 'der Fuhrer' and we took heart. Our misery would end. We would once again assume our role in this world, a world that was not yet ready to accept us. We had to prove ourselves worthy of this role, whether they liked us or not. As much education as one could obtain became a mandate, not a choice. Whatever the new order was to be, we had to attain it, whatever our station in life; we were to perform to the best we were capable of.

"It all sounds reasonable, doesn't it? It surely did back then, and we were all looking for something we could cling to, something we could say was us. Hungry isn't the right word to describe the way we felt. Deprived might be better, although most would have said 'depraved.'

"We needed a scapegoat, and the Jews were the most convenient. It wasn't hard to tie them to what we were experiencing from banking, medicine, even arms manufacturing. They were all about money and the hell with anything else. Get the Jews out of the equation and everything would straighten itself out. Nationality meant nothing to a Jew. He was not a German or a Pole or even an American; he was only after money. To people so desperate, this was the solution. Get rid of the Jews. The message meant sense. The messenger, a voice from God.

"I joined the Hitler Youth. Even my mother encouraged me. My brothers joined as soon as they were of age—Hans almost immediately, Will and Jan shortly after. Foremost in our minds was Trude, one who could have been helped but we didn't have the money. This was personal, as I believe it became for many who chose to follow the same path. There was a reason for our problems and it was the Jews.

"I swallowed all of that and it made sense. Now all I needed to do was do something about it, and 'der Fuhrer' had the answer: get rid of the Jews forever. No one had ever made more sense to me than he did at that moment; it was my patriotic duty, not just to the Fatherland but to the world. I had a duty to perform and nothing should stand in my way.

"I never questioned these men, or what their motives might be or what they stood to gain from this. They were right, and anyone who said they were wrong was the enemy and that enemy was all around us. Almost everyone else said we were wrong, but it only made them that much worse in our minds.

"When we were called upon to join the army, the only danger a man faced was possibly being trampled. Everyone was telling us young men to join up. It was our patriotic duty. And we believed them because we knew it to be true. I did things I will never talk about, but I had orders, and I gave orders, and people died. Not just soldiers, but old men, women, even children.

"In the year before the war ended, I began to realize the truth. Some people were making vast sums of money, probably deposited in Swiss bank accounts, off our blood and from those we were killing. There was nothing patriotic about what we were doing. The ones who called themselves patriots were little more than ghouls, profiting off the blood of those they encouraged. How many of them would tell their sons or grandsons to join in service to the Fatherland? 'No, stay here and help me make the weapons that others will use against the enemy. We'll get even wealthier.'

"I killed many people, far too many. I wish I could say they were all soldiers, but they were not. Well before the end of the war I had killed enough. I was sick, sick in the heart. I had seen enough violence and blood. I did whatever I could to avoid conflict. I even aimed to miss." He took another swig of beer, a drop sliding down his cheek. He needed the beer, the catharsis coming easier with help from the alcohol. "Stettin was overrun by the Russians. I never heard from my mother again after her last letter in '44. My brothers, all of them, even sixteen-year-old Willie, served on the Eastern Front. I never heard a word from them after they finished training. They just went and disappeared. I tried to find out what happened but all I found was the dates they had boarded the trains, not when or if they returned. So few returned. I suppose it is possible one or more of them survived but it was impossible to find out without jeopardizing myself. I suppose, in that regard, I am a coward." He took another long pull on his beer. "When I did the math, I realized that Willie and Jan could not have had the same father as me. Mama had a friend or maybe was helping out the family in another way. Willie was the youngest by many years.

"I decided it was time to save myself. I was a criminal—not in my mind, but in the minds of those who thought themselves normal through all the insanity." He spoke directly to Hank. "My son, I hope with all my heart you will never know the depth of my despair over what I have done. Your mother, now gone almost ten years, died without ever knowing the truth about me or my past. She was a saint and I the worst kind of sinner. I lied, even to her. We met in a camp for Displaced Persons, DPs we were called. We were people who had been uprooted by the war and had no place to return. Like many of the SS I had the emblem tattooed on my arm. I managed to burn it out and obliterate the whole area, claiming to have been burned trying to save a family from a burning house, getting injured but saving at least a woman and her daughter. The incident never happened but the daughter was your mother, Hans, and she backed up the story. Her mother was so incoherent she could have said anything and it might have been true, at least believably true. That's all that mattered.

"We were married in the camp in '46. Your grandmother—I believe she really was your grandmother though at times your mother treated her as though she was no relation at all, she was so out of her mind—died less than a month after we were married.

"We lived in the camp almost as if it was to be where we would spend the rest of our lives. I was in constant fear the Allies would learn of my identity and I would be sent off to a prison for whatever remained of my miserable life, but somehow it did not happen, though it should have. I would have accepted the punishment, not for what I did but for my stupidity, for having thought it was my duty, duty to be a fool.

"Duty... duty to do what? To give reason for someone who already has more money than he can spend to make even more? Is it my duty to help other young men suffer wounds so deep they cannot be seen and then just turn them loose in society where they wreak havoc with behavior no one who has not been in combat can understand? Killing to remain alive is not one of mankind's higher ideals. It may be necessary at times but should not be what we strive for. I chose to live, to live to try to make right what I had made wrong, and it happened.

"As Displaced Persons we were divvied up among the victors in the war. Your mother and I, and you, your mother now carrying you, had to decide between Australia and America. I thought Australia was better. We could simply get lost in the confusion of an emerging nation. Your mother insisted on America, and she won. The rest, we can say, is history.

"If there is one thing I can say that I hope you will take to your heart, both of you: question anyone who says it is your duty to do anything. He may have a motive not apparent. A legal term, I don't know what it is in Latin, says, 'Who benefits?' It is a question one should ask when someone says it is your duty. If it is your duty, why is it not his?

"If you are told it is your *patriotic duty* you should be especially on your toes. After what I have been through and what countless others all over this world have been through, if someone says, 'It is your patriotic duty,' I say that is the person you shoot first. Let the other enemies wait. Get the worst one out of the way first."

I was blown out of my mind. Hank was shaken to the core. He had never known his father's past. His mother had died while he was still in high school, but he knew they were both wartime refugees. They had made the best of the opportunities that had come their way and he was the result. The dream of education had been beyond their grasp, but they had given it to him. As far as the past was concerned, it was over and done with. The rest was up to him. If he chose to tell the story, so be it. If not, it was to rest where it lay.

I gave Hank my word I would not utter a word of his father's story and till this day I have not. Hank's father died less than two years after that memorable evening. I left the teaching profession about the same time, concentrating my efforts on the farm. Less than a year ago, almost forty years later, I received word that Hank had also passed away. A mutual friend relayed that Hank, although married twice, never had any children. For nearly all these forty years since that reckoning, he had lived and then died in the Syracuse area. At the time of his passing, from cancer, he was in the middle of his second divorce. His drinking had gotten the best of him and that was the reason for divorce. I often wonder which caused the problem, the drinking or the knowledge of the past.

I agonized over whether to write this piece. I had given my word and for the whole time I knew Hank was alive I kept it. To my knowledge there is no one left who will be affected by sharing this story here. All the main characters are gone, except possibly the divorcees, and I sincerely doubt they were ever told the story. The old man never mentioned it again and there is the possibility that the whole thing may have been made up, the ramblings of an inebriated old fool. I never thought of him as a fool and I still don't. It may have taken the alcohol to give him the courage to come right out with it, or he might have had some inkling of the disease that shortly would take him.

That evening was one of the first times I had heard someone use the saying that, "We should question authority." I had heard it before but always from the mouths of younger, protesting hippie types, easily disregarded by most. But the old man's message rings true. When someone says you have a "patriotic duty" to risk your life, ask him why he is not risking his own or that of his children, even grandchildren. Hemingway had it right when he described war. War wasn't about the glory of killing thousands of the enemy and returning to a cheering crowd. War was voices, one at a time asking, "Doctor, will I ever see again? Will I ever walk? Will I be able to have children?" That's what war is. That is, if you survive.

I owe a great deal to the old man and Hank. They helped make me a citizen of the world. The simpler a person's station in life, the more I respect him. Exalted ones beware: I tend to look at you with an air of skepticism, and I will question your motivation. What do you seek to gain and at whose expense?

Is Anybody Home?

When I was younger, some might say more enthusiastic, it was not unusual for me and others to work absurd hours. Not seeing a bed for two or even three days was the rule if an important task needed finishing. For example, back-to-back trips to the Boston Produce Terminal with loads of beans, potatoes, corn, or whatever became a necessary evil if prices held. A sixty-hour week meant you took a day off for some holiday or fatigue finally caught up with you. Eighty to one hundred hours was the norm.

I had a young, growing family back then and found myself driven to provide in the best way I knew how. Translated, this meant I worked as hard and as smart as I could. I felt I was providing them with everything needed.

But I wasn't.

An essential ingredient in my children's growth process was being left by the wayside: Dad.

Martha, my wife, was on my case, but since there always seemed to be a pressing matter, the idea of spending more time with the kids found itself moved to the back burner more often than deserved. Though I don't believe my marriage was ever in any danger (Martha must be some kind of saint), I know of marriages that have suffered as a result of not finding time for anything other than work.

I absolutely loved my family, let no one doubt that. My most cherished memories are of times the old station wagon (the kids later called it The Battle-Wagon) would come bouncing along a farm road with lunch and a pile of kids (neighbors included) for a picnic lunch on the farm. I can picture those days like yesterday, and God, they were the stuff from which legends were born.

It was too easy, casual if you will, to put the subject off when Martha would bring it up, but when my almost five-year-old daughter wanted to cuddle and I had to go back to work, it really hit home.

"Daddy, we don't see you anymore." She was right; I was gone before they were awake and not home until they were already in bed. Martha was a damn good mother to those kids, despite their dad's absence. I was in danger of becoming the parent to only be feared. "Just wait until your father gets home..." didn't seem to carry much weight if they were already in bed by the time Dad found the time to get there.

But those words from my daughter hit home more than all the appeals from my wife. I had to go, others were expecting me, but the tears and the pleading could not be ignored. Again, she would be asleep before I came home that night, but I had to finish arrangements for tomorrow's market trip. I made the dreaded promise to a child, "Tomorrow I will come home early, and we will all go out to 'Friendly's' for ice cream, okay?"

She was thrilled and jumped into my arms. The adventure and anticipation spoke more than I could have imagined. Martha later told me that little Christine was watching out for her daddy most of the day. It meant that much.

The next day, I arranged for Mark, my foreman, to take the load to Boston. I was whipped but at least I could go home for a few hours to rest before starting with the whole game all over again. I was a little earlier, but not much. The kids were still up, waiting. Martha had let them stay because they insisted that we were going out for ice cream "when Daddy gets home," and Daddy was home.

Martha was all smiles at me as the kids danced around. This was the moment, but all I could think about was somehow getting into a horizontal position. I didn't want to eat, drink or anything. All I wanted was rest for an extremely fatigued body.

I had forgotten about the promise made to my "Daddy-deprived" kids. But they remembered.

"Daddy needs a few minutes to rest," I said while easing my way onto the couch. Martha did call the kids off and I had almost fallen asleep. But a promise made to a child is a promise one must keep. I doubt more than five minutes passed before I heard the first plaintive cry from up close, "Daddy, please."

I don't remember if I even moved, but through a narrow slit I saw my three children standing there in front of me—Keith, the youngest, still in diapers; Jen, the daughter who for most of her younger years reminded me of the cartoon character, "Dondi;" and Christine, the five-year-old going on twenty-five, the manipulator. It was Christine. "Daddy, please... Daddy, please..." The others knew she was the boss, the leader of the pack, the family pack.

I pretended sleep, but there was no way, and the kids knew it. The more I wanted to sleep, the more I heard, "Daddy, please... Daddy, please..." The younger ones started to repeat, most likely by rote. How do you ignore something like that, even if you feel dead on your feet? I tried, because I was at the end of the rope, but then came the *coup de grâce* from Christine.

She reached over with a tiny hand and carefully opened one of my eyes by the lashes, looked deeply into my eye (how could I not see her?) and asked, "Is anybody home?"

Is anybody home? How do you ignore that question from your child? I don't care how worn out you might think you are, and I was close to dead, you will summon another level of strength and make the experience count. I put on the best face possible, perhaps only pretending to be awake, and we all piled into the old Battle Wagon to go to Friendly's for ice cream. Martha had to drive. I did not feel competent, but I felt a lot better as Daddy.

It takes a child to teach an adult how to be a good parent. There are things in life more important than the pursuit of material goods. No amount of money or things can make up for the absence of influence that Mom or Dad can have on their kids. No one should ever have to worry whether they are good enough. YOU ARE THE BEST PARENTS THEY HAVE. The act of being there when needed is all that it takes.

Words of wisdom often come from the mouths of babes. As the so-called adults in the room, it behooves us to pay more attention to those to whom we plan to pass the torch. The teenager from Sweden, Greta Thunberg, immediately comes to mind. What kind of mess will this next generation inherit because we failed to listen and do anything about it?

When it's all over—when they are grown, off on their own—there is little more you can do. Don't be the one who is asked, "Was anybody home?" Regarding my children, I like to think I woke up in time. We all need to wake up and listen a little more.

Sandra Day O'Dawg

It had been a particularly bad week as far as the family pets went. Sambo, the black and white cat used up the last of his nine lives crossing the road in front of the house and Muffie—no, not the vampire slayer, but our perfect Golden Retriever, except she was black—died under the juniper bushes out front of the house. We think she was killed by a car also. The police called me to ask if we had seen a wounded bear in the neighborhood. A motorist reported having hit one near my house. Muffie weighed over 130 pounds and looked a lot like a bear.

Sambo was a great cat. He followed you around like a dog, pardon the expression. Constantly rubbing himself up against all of his family, we were all well marked, even Muffie. They never fought like "cats and dogs." It was indeed a bad day when they were both gone.

Enter one Josie Slavinski. Josie and I had known each other for years—more as casual acquaintances than friends—but when she became a salesperson for WSBS we had reason to see each other on more or less a regular basis. In those days I did a lot of advertising on the radio and Josie was a damn good salesperson. She also had the misfortune of being the one whose car hit Sambo.

You can train a dog to be wary of the road and the vehicles that speed by, but you can't train a cat. They're too damn independent, a trait that more often than not leads to their demise. Josie felt badly. She had known Muffie. The dog had been my constant companion, and she had seen and petted her many times. Muffie was a most lovable dog, rumored to have "the fastest tongue in the west."

Although there was nothing she could have done, Josie felt terrible about having been somewhat responsible for the death of the remaining family pet. But she found an answer. Her neighbor's Golden Retriever had just given birth to a litter of ten pups. All were sold except the runt. There's always a runt of the litter. And that's how Sandy forever changed our lives.

She was small, a lot smaller than her brothers and sisters, but she possessed an intelligence level I doubt any ever matched. Of all the dogs I have ever known, either by ownership or association, I have never known one who could tell you not only what she wanted but knew when you were having a bad time and what to do to get you back on a positive track. She was a positive influence no matter what was happening.

The story goes that Harry Truman had a hard time during his presidency. Not only had he been the one who authorized the dropping of the atomic bomb on Japan, but now, in the midst of the Korean conflict, he had to fire the most popular general in modern history. History says his positive "poll numbers" were somewhere around nineteen percent. A reporter supposedly asked him if he was concerned about these low numbers. His response: "Son, in this town, if you need a friend, get a dog."

Sandy—that's what the kids decided to call her—was never a problem. She never wet the floor or soiled the carpet as a pup. Everything she had to do she did outside. She was part of the family from day one but never begged at the table, although I'm sure she probably received scraps from all of us at one time or another. She was just too cute and irresistible.

Despite her lack of size, we were told she should be registered with the AKC because she was a purebred. We were set on the name Sandy, but it seemed every variation of the name had already been taken. It was just about this time that Sandra Day O'Connor was appointed to the U.S. Supreme Court, but alas, even that name was already taken. Thus, Sandy became Sandra Day O'Dawg, at least as far as the AKC was concerned.

It was almost as if Sandy knew of the irony connected with her name. She grew rapidly, gaining as much in intelligence as body size. Human vocabulary was never a problem to this dog. Every move we made, either as individuals or as a family, seemed anticipated. If we ever had to leave her at home, she let you know she was disappointed, and frequently she won out, happy to be in the back seat with the kids.

"Born to play," was her motto. Her toys could be found almost everywhere in the house, but you knew her favorites. A little squeaky mouse she would crunch endlessly to get our attention seemed most attractive. She wanted us to hide this noisemaker to see if she could find it, which of course she always could, even if we were sitting on it. Sandy was strong enough she could upset us, the chair, couch, and coffee table, and come up with her treasure. More than once her tail cleared the coffee table with one wag.

Sandy was never far from the action. She would accompany me to the farm store every morning and greet each of the employees as a long-lost friend. She knew where the boxes of bones were kept and who the easy "marks" were. She was never hungry, for she had too many friends.

When Sandy wanted a bone, she would always find something to trade for it. It might be an old cash register receipt or the order form that was lying on top of a pallet waiting for pick up. She was always helping us, even if our orders got mixed up as a result. Of course, she always got a bone. How could anyone resist? Some invoices had a little dog juice on them. No one complained.

Retrieving was Sandy's destiny. Whether it was the mouse, a stick, or a simple rock, it was her duty to go find and fetch it. No matter where we tossed or hid the thing, she would find it, even if it weighed several pounds.

The Town of Great Barrington brought many giant truckloads of autumn leaves for composting. One day my son Keith, whether in an attempt to keep the dog busy or by accident, tossed a stone into the midst of this monumental leaf pile. Of course, the more the dog went after the illusive rock, the deeper it sank into the pile of leaves, but she persisted. All day long she kept digging after her stone, but it kept sinking. Leaves flew this way and that, and often she was buried out of sight inside a hole of truly massive proportions. Determination proved to be her strong suit and by the end of the day, a truly exhausted dog presented Keith with the stone he had thrown. It was simply her job and it would take more than some hard work to keep her from doing it.

I did a lot of hayrides for children in those days, and Sandy became a constant fixture. At first, she would trot just ahead of the tractor. My passengers became convinced Sandy was going to be crushed by the tractor at any moment, but it never happened. As she grew older, Sandy preferred to ride on the wagon with the children. At first she jumped up, but in her later years we had to lift her. Nonetheless, it was her job to entertain and she performed well almost until the end.

Goldens tend to have shorter life spans, as dogs go. Eight to ten years is the norm. Sandy was more than twelve before difficulties began. At first it was arthritis, especially in the hips. Treatments helped but more than one veterinarian told us it was time to put her down. There was no way any one of us could allow our best friend to die like that. So we all did our share of carrying her up and down the stairs when necessary. The pain she endured was evident, but she never complained. To the contrary, after each time she was helped, Sandy would look us in the eye and, in her own way, say, "Thank you."

Time went on but her condition never improved. There was nothing wrong with her that five years younger wouldn't fix, but she never failed to thank those who helped her… up to the end

She was nearly sixteen, almost double the age she could normally have expected to attain, when things took a dramatic turn for the worst. She could no longer walk more than a few steps without trouble and had to be carried from her bed do her business outside. There was never a mess. She always gave a signal when she needed help, and there was always someone there to help. We owed her that.

One day, Keith helped her out and back onto her bed again. It was plain to all that her time was limited but no one would deny her a minute of it. Most of the crew, her friends, gathered in the back room for lunch. Sandy was the topic of discussion.

She knew it was time.

With a supreme effort, Sandy lifted her head off her bed and made extended eye contact with every person in the room one at a time. All conversation ceased; you could hear the proverbial pin drop. Then she put her head back down, closed her eyes, and left this world forever.

For the rest of that day and several days after that, not a dry eye was seen at the farm. Much of the staff said they felt worse after Sandy's death than after humans they knew had passed away. The only emotion Sandy had ever shown for anyone was love, and she displayed it up to the end.

We buried her by the pine trees near my home. Her home. She spent much time there playing with the children. I see the place just about every day. It's near the well where I have to go to get water for the chickens. I find myself thinking about her when times are trying. To quote Mark Twain: "If you pick up a starving dog and make him prosperous, he will not bite you. This is the principal difference between a dog and a man."

Sandy was one hell of a dog, far better than a lot of the humans I've known.

Angel of the Night

I know of no rational adult human being who can say he has never experienced an unexplainable event. Some might claim the inexplicable as an almost expected occurrence, but not me. I'm not big on the idea of spirituality, ghosts, or visits from anything otherworldly. I find no fault with those that do, but there have been times when events or appearances have left my jaw on the floor. Skeptical I remain, but I've learned to leave room for exceptions.

One significant occurrence was the very first time I saw the woman to whom I have now been married for more than fifty years. When I saw her, I knew she was the one, but I had to earn her. There was never a question in my mind, though she may have had several and looking back, I wouldn't blame her. I was little more than a social idiot, having spent way too much time in a seminary-like environment. Four children and seven grandchildren later, I hope she still feels she made the right choice. I know I did.

The feeling that took over my mind that day back in 1963 was something like I have never felt before or since. I knew, and I just had to make it happen. What some would call "other worldly experiences" has happened from time to time. Now I am more reflective, but when I was younger, and perhaps more enthusiastic, I had my "green mist" times out on the farm, as I recounted in the Introduction. On three occasions while in my fields I found myself surrounded by a vaporous substance, call it a green fog, that mystifies but leaves you with a sense of contentment the likes of which I have never experienced. You feel a validation for what you are doing from something far greater than any given by mankind. I have spoken with farmers from across the country that have had similar experiences. It's hard to describe, but mind-blowing when it happens.

There have been times when I felt communication with another, someone who knew my intentions or wanted to help in a difficult moment. I'm sure many have experienced the occasion someone anticipated what you were going to say or do. Whether the result of a good guess or ESP, who knows.

In 1985, I was invited to a farm conference in Des Moines, Iowa. The event was national, even international in scope. Concerned with the direct marketing of farm products right to consumers, thousands of farmers from the U.S. and several foreign countries attended. It was all about eliminating middlemen and making a few extra dollars for the farmer, perhaps the difference in the game of survival, while saving the consumer money. Presentations, seminars, and informal gatherings took place from dawn to well into the night, even during mealtimes. It was impossible to take all this in no matter how you tried. Sometimes luck smiled and you could trade notes with an acquaintance that had attended a seminar you had missed but often you just had to make the choice. It happened more than once.

As much as I might have tried, I found myself missing a lot of insightful seminars and regretting it. On the Wednesday morning of this week-long event, I was mired in the dilemma once again but this time I heard a voice, a female voice, saying not to worry, I should go to the seminar on "Value-added products" and she would attend the one dealing with storage crops and retail marketing of the same. I had not talked to a soul about which, if any, of the seminars I had chosen to attend. None in sight was paying any inordinate kind of attention to me, but the voice came through loud and clear again, "I'll meet with you during the lunch break." I saw no one remotely even looking at me, but it was time to go.

I took as many notes as my distracted mind would allow. Just who was this mystery woman that managed to get inside my head? I hadn't the faintest idea.

No attempt to communicate with me was made for the next two hours, two more seminars. Just as the last one broke I heard from her again, "Save me a seat next to you. You don't know me but don't worry, I'll find you. I hope you have good notes."

I had no idea what was happening but, why not? Play along, see what happens. Luncheon tables varied in size from large groups to those seating just a few. Two men, one of whom I knew (Alan Wilson from Lexington, Massachusetts), were sitting together at one of the tables for four. Alan motioned me to join them.

It still left a seat for the mystery guest, whoever she might be. Alan introduced me to his companion, Jim Hightower, the Commissioner of Agriculture from the State of Texas, one of the wittiest, smartest, and most entertaining men I have ever met. Mr. Hightower, Jim he insisted, had Alan and me in stitches from the moment he opened his mouth. The guy could have been a stand-up comic; the problem was everything he said was true.

It was during this rollicking good time that I felt a hand on my shoulder. I looked up to see this older black-haired, dark-complexioned woman smiling at me as she asked if she might join the group. A total stranger to all of us, but her voice was the one I had heard in my head. If not old enough to be my mother she was easily as old as my older sister, but certainly younger in attitude than either.

We talked little with the mystery woman during lunch, though I caught both Jim and Alan giving her an occasional glance as Jim kept us laughing. Nothing could stop Jim, a natural comic, and our guest laughed as much as anyone. She did introduce herself, though I fail to remember her name now more than thirty years later. For the sake of the story we'll call her Debbie, and I do remember she was from a small town in Minnesota. Later, Alan asked me what I knew about Debbie. He said he kept having these strange feelings about this woman, like he knew her from somewhere in the past.

The lunch break was always two hours in length for two reasons. One, the crowd was so large they had two servings, and secondly, the thousands in attendance wanted time to see the trade show in the auditorium next door.

I could have listened to Jim Hightower for hours. The laughter he created was the best incentive for digestion ever invented, but we had to make room for the next wave. As we shook hands, Alan gave me an unmistakable look and whispered, "What's going on? I want to talk with you later."

I nodded and then went off with Debbie, who had her notes out already. Lunch might have been a good time, but this gal was all business. "What's new?"

We compared notes, talked about which conferences we were each going to attend and where we agreed to meet to exchange notes. At one point she smiled at me and said, "Don't even think about it; I'm too old, my husband trusts me, and your wife loves you." End of story. Almost. We continued to exchange notes for the duration of the conference, I hope to both our benefits. She gave me a kiss at the airport as she flew off to Minnesota and Alan gave me the third degree as to just what the hell was happening. He said he felt most uncomfortable whenever she was around, like she was inside his head. She was in mine, that I know.

I begged off with Alan, saying I felt uncomfortable as well but somehow attracted. I never did tell him about the communication. I don't know if I ever really did understand what was going on. I received a letter from Debbie some weeks later, apologetic for interfering with my mind... Also to thank me for my help at the conference. I returned a letter in kind and have heard nothing from her since, either by mail or by any other form of communication. I wish her nothing but the best. From what Alan told me, Debbie had an unsettling effect on others at the conference as well.

• • •

Debbie is not the only one I have heard from without speaking. There have been a number, some more significant than others.

A few have been profound, though most have been oblique, at least in affectation.

An incident happened back in the 1990s that came back to haunt me (no other way to describe it) many years later. Martha has been the love of my life, always has been, always will be. We have always shared the same bed, rarely ever been apart. Both of us read, often late into the night, especially if we're into a novel or a story. I had turned my light off first and rolled over. She was still reading.

Hours later, I never looked at the clock, I awoke to see a woman standing at the foot of our bed. I am near-sighted, but I know there was a woman in our bedroom, though she didn't seem to move from the place I first saw her. Martha's light was still on; I thought maybe she had gone to the bathroom and was standing near the bed but when I glanced over, I saw she had fallen asleep, the book still in her hands. When I reached out to put on my glasses, the woman was still there. For at least ten seconds I got a good look at her face and features, her dress appearing old, possibly antique, but very formal, just before she dissolved into thin air, smiling at me the whole time.

I told Martha about it in the morning after not sleeping a wink. She dismissed it as a dream and for years the whole incident never crossed my mind.

Years passed, more than twenty of them, the whole thing relegated to an obscure zone of memory. Then one day a female employee at the farm approached me with an intriguing thought. A friend of hers was putting together a one-woman show about a historical figure named Helen Andrews. Because I had a little experience with theater (college level only), she asked if I could help her with the production. I was most under-qualified but since I was the only one with any kind of experience they knew, I said okay.

But just who the hell was Helen Andrews? Helen Andrews was the wife and widow of Thomas Andrews, the chief designer and builder of *RMS Titanic*. He went down with the ship in 1912. Now it started getting interesting. Denise, the girl who was performing, was a distant relative of Helen Andrews, born the day Helen Andrews died. She had a remarkable resemblance to the real Helen and, quite frankly, gave me a strange feeling from time to time.

I worked with her, with my limited capacity and knowledge, and witnessed the growth of a truly gifted actress. In the short time I was with her, I witnessed her transformation into another person altogether. She became Helen Andrews, and I became very uneasy. At one venue, the uneasiness reached its climax. Denise often displayed life-sized cutouts of Helen and her husband, Thomas. The cutout of Helen appeared to smile at me from every angle. I couldn't escape her gaze. It was the woman I had seen in my bedroom years prior. I was in no way mistaken. It was her; even the dress worn in one of the photos appeared the same as the one worn in the bedroom that night. Haunting, chilling... to say the least.

Shortly thereafter, I received a certified letter from Denise, inspired no doubt by her friend, now a former employee, that said she no longer wanted to see me. There was little explanation. She threatened me with legal action if I ever set foot on the property where she lived. I have never received definitive explanation for this line of behavior. I have no idea what the legal action may have been, nor did I feel any need to inquire. Besides, I couldn't give her any further training, for I wasn't qualified. I haven't talked to Denise, the former employee, or Helen Andrews since, but I wish them all well.

• • •

Perhaps one of the strangest happenings occurred only three years prior to my meeting Denise. My doctor diagnosed me with BPH, Benign Prostate Hyperplasia, and a swollen prostate gland. This gave me intense pain every time I went to urinate—pure torture. After non-surgical treatment gave little results, we scheduled an operation with full knowledge of possible consequences.

Coming out of the surgery, I was in la-la land—painkillers

to the max. Your brain might not register the pain but your body, your mind, does. My body felt nothing, but the rest of me knew something was not right; in fact, something was wrong.

Restraints are in place to ensure limited movement. A catheter was inserted, and to be certain it didn't come out, they inflated a balloon within my bladder. To keep the catheter in the right position, my penis was held in traction… Oh my God.

God only knew what they injected to keep the pain away, but somehow my body knew, and there was no way to turn that knowledge off. I was flat on my back, unable to move, wired for sound. Sleep was impossible, drugs only keeping me from descending to the next lower level of insanity.

Then there was the matter of my roommate. He had also had surgery, done through his nose. He had to remain motionless for his passages to heal. Until then, he had to remain flat on his back, breathe only through his mouth, and snore. Oh, my God did he snore! His drugs were meant to keep him asleep all the time, but that meant constant snoring! I never knew anyone could be that loud. It was as if a large diesel engine was exhausting into a sound amplifier.

Sleep was impossible. For most of the next three days I could not doze more than a few minutes. Visits from my doctor or nurses, well-intentioned friends, orderlies, or just noise had me wired. Noise, like the excruciating inhuman blasts coming from the erratically running, un-muffled engine in the bed next to me ensured there was just no way. If I slept at all it wasn't because I slept. It was because I had passed out from exhaustion with possible help from whatever was dripping into my veins. I was focused on watching the hands of a clock on the wall. Daytime television, I became convinced, was somehow a conspiracy between the healthcare industry and the "entertainment" moguls to first make you sick and then keep you sick in order to give otherwise unemployed actors and orderlies a reason to get up in the morning. This was one of the most agonizing, desperate low points of my life. If someone had given me a gun, I might have used it on myself.

At some time during the depths of my third night in the hospital, I reached the breaking point. It was impossible to imagine a human able to make the kind of noise my companion made. It was as if he was shouting, no, *screaming* his snores. To avoid reopening the wounds from his surgery, all things were being administered and removed through tubes in his arms and elsewhere.

The day nurse had said they were trying to wean me off the drugs, and I was feeling the pain almost to its full extent. I was ready to castrate myself if it would have helped. It would be hard for me to say that I had even approached a state of sleep for more than a couple of hours in total since surgery three days ago.

I rang for the nurse. After three days and nights I had come to recognize each one, but the person who answered my call was a new face. Everyone had been professional, courteous, and sympathetic to my unreal situation as conditions warranted. I had no complaints, but this woman was different. Her smile somehow told me she knew what I was going through, as if she too, felt the pain. Another major difference stood out, something unmistakable. She was dressed as if she was from the fifties or sixties, not the nineties. Her hair was teased up into a "bouffant," and her uniform had shoulder-pads. She appeared to be in her mid-fifties, like me, and I got a clear look at her nametag. That name is burned forever in my memory: Roberta Dunlop.

I first asked if anything could be done for my roommate. The noise was so loud we had difficulty conversing, forced to repeat ourselves. She tried to help him but was more concerned with me. If it could be considered any kind of comfort, they had complaints of the snoring from as far as two rooms away. He was that loud. She could increase the painkiller if I wanted, but it would not help me sleep. She had two other calls, but if I could find a way to roll onto my side she would come back and massage my back with powder to help me relax. I might be able to gain a little legitimate sleep.

I did manage, and she did come back. I remember her touch and the feeling of relief unlike anything I have ever experienced. The snoring lessened, then faded, and I passed into a most restful dreamless sleep. Eighteen hours later I woke up, hungry and close to pain-free. The catheters were still in place, but now they felt only uncomfortable rather than painful. The bed next to me was empty, and my doctor told me I was due to be released the next morning. I was completely off the painkillers. They asked if I would like dinner.

The ordeal was over, almost. From there it was all recovery mode. When the night shift nurse came in for a check, it was the regular nurse I had seen the nights before. I asked about the duty nurse from the previous night.

"I worked last night. I've worked every night since you've been here," she responded.

"Well, thank you for rubbing me down, helping me to sleep."

"Your thanks are accepted, but I never rubbed you. You were already asleep when I came in on my regular check. Exhaustion must have done you in. Your roommate was unbelievable. They finally moved him to a private room, probably sound-proofed."

I wasn't going to give up. "Well, please thank nurse Dunlop for me."

She shook her head. "There's no one by that name working this floor, not that I know of."

"Roberta Dunlop. Light-haired, fiftyish, smile that could melt an iceberg, really concerned about everyone..."

I might have touched a nerve unintentionally.

"We're all concerned. About everyone. That's why we're nurses," she said. "I have never heard of a nurse by that name in this hospital." With that she gave me the programmed smile and walked out of the room.

The required ride in the wheelchair was given by a different nurse the following morning. As casually as seemed appropriate, I asked for my sincere thanks to be extended to nurse Roberta Dunlop. The gal behind the chair calmly responded that she had never heard of this nurse but would check the registry. Almost a week later I had a message on my answering machine from her. No one knew of this nurse. Could I have made a mistake?

I know the name I saw on her tag. It's not as if there could have been a spelling mistake. There had been powder on my back and in my bed when I awoke that evening. The day nurses even asked about it. Whatever happened, happened. Who did it and where she came from might be debatable, but the powder remained as evidence.

The name Roberta Dunlop is a fictitious name. I have made it up for the sake of this story. But the person was real. I have researched the real name on the Internet and come up empty. I wondered who she was and how we may have been connected.

• • •

I am at a stage now when most of my life is composed of memories, but it's not over yet. Each year, as the holiday season approaches, the farm takes on employees to help through the times when a plastic smiley face is essential no matter how tired, exhausted, or otherwise dead on your feet you may feel. Christmas orders have a way of becoming emergencies for the socialites screaming into your phone. "But I must have it by Thursday. The decorators will be here by then. The guests will start arriving on Friday. Do you understand what that means?"

Oh, yes, we understand; we of lesser means are trying to take care of our families through the winter. Do you know what that means?

We try to accommodate everyone, from those who just wish to decorate the family grave to the woman who absolutely must make sure the palace is perfect. To do so we hire extras for the holiday season. Shari was one of these. Though she claimed to be a local, I'd never met her before, but as I backed the truck in to where the staff was waiting, I felt a presence, something I'd felt before, something I recognized; a special person was waiting.

I hardly wanted to say hello, even after I was first introduced. I had never met her before, and honestly, I was scared. I knew there was a connection of some sort but had no idea what it might be. The next few weeks were going to be interesting.

Martha is, and always has been, the love of my life, no question. Others have tried to intrude on our relationship, but none has taken her place. Sometimes they were only asking advice from me. I have tried to help, hopefully succeeded, in helping some of them reach a settlement, others just to become happy, maybe less fearful.

Shari was one of these, ready to make a leap into the unknown, divorce, but unsure of the consequences. Whatever I could do I did to help her on a course never contemplated. I have come to feel a responsibility to those who make contact, though sometimes they may never speak a word.

Other than a hug or two, Shari and I never had any kind of intimate contact. Contact, yes. We spoke to one another frequently as she tried to straighten her life out in North Carolina. I felt she was too emotionally involved with possessions down South. Did she still own them? As it turned out, she may not have. The Berkshires had a much larger claim on her soul.

It would be hard for me to say that Shari's soul was connected to mine, but there is something I cannot explain. As I age, and I am considerably older than her, I feel aches and pains, ailments never contemplated in younger years. On a few occasions, after inquiring, she has been able by force of will, I believe, to alleviate if not eliminate the problem. She claims to have the ability to help even many miles from the recipient. I can't speak for the distance, often from as far away as North Carolina, but she has certainly helped my aches and pains without any form of physical contact.

• • •

By no means have all my "unusual" contacts been female. Years ago, an elderly gentleman approached me at one of the farmer's markets where I sometimes sell goods. Harold had a passion for the coleus plant, and I had a considerable collection at this market. As he and his wife moved among my stock, I overheard him describing them by their Latin names, saying he had this one out by the patio or that one was something he had never seen before. But coleus was his passion; his desire for the plant was endless, almost religious in nature.

Something clicked. I had never been that attracted to the species, but I did like it and there seemed a great number of varieties and rainbow of colors. Harold was the official ambassador of Coleus Nation. Over the few years I was fortunate enough to know him, we became close friends, sometimes sharing a drink or two and conversation between good friends. I learned a great deal about the coleus plant, and life, from a man who had endured the pain of growing up poor in New York with no direction in life and then finding himself in combat in Korea. Coming home after his service, a compass emerged in his listless life and he went on to establish one of the largest wholesale electrical supply houses in the country. He was not a poor man.

I confessed to never having figured out why, although classified as 1A through most of the Vietnam conflict, I had never been drafted.

"Because it was meant to be," he replied. "We were meant to meet and talk about much more than coleus."

Over the next five years we would meet whenever possible and share a little philosophy on life. Harold was well on in his years, and though he had several children of his own he confessed to finding it easier talking with me than with any of his adult kids.

I dearly loved this man who, never having had an education beyond high school, was undoubtedly one of the most intelligent human beings on this planet. Intelligence is not to be measured by one's level of education, but one's ability to see what is really going on and at least make some attempt to fix it. Harold had this ability better than any individual I have ever known. But his time was running out, and he knew it.

Just after Labor Day a few years ago, I was packing up after another farmer's market. I heard Harold's voice in my head imploring me to come to his house. I've been there before but always following his lead. "Don't worry, the guard at the gate knows you're coming." He lived in a gated retirement community.

I trusted my instincts. The guard at Harold's gated community just waved me through, though I was driving a truck. Harold was waiting just outside his garage. We embraced, as often happened, and he proceeded to explain why he contacted me so surreptitiously.

"You and I are a lot alike. I knew it the moment I met you. This is probably the last time we will ever see one another in this life. Joan and I are on our way to our place in Florida. She is ill and I have received a lousy diagnosis as well. We've had our dance and neither of us has regrets. This is the Big Goodbye and I want to give you some things I will no longer need, and maybe you will remember me with."

With that he proceeded to load up my truck with all manner of things—tools, books, artifacts from places he had visited. When I protested that at least some of these things should go to his children, he scoffed. "They'll just throw them out in a few years and anything they ever meant will be forgotten. When you read one of these books or use this shovel, maybe you will think of me."

It was one of the hardest farewells I have ever had to endure. We embraced and we both cried.

Last spring in 2019, I heard from a mutual friend that Joan had passed away, and a week later Harold joined her. A man couldn't have had a better mentor and friend.

• • •

There have been others, both people and incidents, all of which have influenced my being in one form or another. The encounters are sometimes brief but the effects long lasting. I believe there is a form of communication we all share to some extent, with some more than others. Perhaps it is in our evolutionary future that this species, not known for its ability to get along, will finally reach its potential for true understanding. But it will take time and work. Certainly luck must be involved.

I still can't say I believe in ghosts of any type. I prefer to say there is a lot more to be learned and it will take a long time. Then, and only then, will we be able to say and humbly understand that we will never know it all.

Tales From the Farm

The Farm

Back in the fifties, I had been growing vegetables for a number of years already, mostly just to put a few dollars away for a future education, I hoped, but there seemed to be the "think small" problem when it came to making the real bucks necessary to get the job done. If I was to ever obtain the dollars needed to really make it into college, much less an institution claiming a reasonably elite level, I had to do a little more. At that time, no one from my family had ever graduated from college other than an uncle who had become a priest.

When some of my more energetic friends boasted of having saved close to a hundred dollars or more after a summer's labors, I realized I had to go a step further if I was to attain the goals I had set for myself. The potential was there, people wanted what I grew, but I didn't have the expertise or the physical ability to carry it to the next level. I just couldn't do it on my own. The long-term future was obscured by the real and present. As a youngster, I was caught up in the race for space; the technology gap that seemed to separate us from the Russians just as much as I failed to recognize that I would have to do something different if I wanted to attain my goals and influence change.

I had read and largely understood most things about the "Space Race" but had neglected to learn the practical knowledge about the means to gain the education to get into that race. I think I read everything Werner Van Braun ever wrote about rocketry, but I never even knew the University of Massachusetts had an extension service for farmers; from a later perspective, I have to say the two were interlinked. The higher goal of technology could never be attained unless the near-term knowledge of agriculture was somehow to be obtained.

I continued doing what my family had always done—we grew what we needed plus a little more and sold off the extra, with a few things added just for kicks. One of the things added was strawberries. The first year we made the crop it was spectacular. The next year we were hit with a late frost and everything we had worked for was gone in the course of one night. I learned rather quickly that the greater the potential rewards, the greater the risk, and the more likelihood you could lose your shirt. Minimizing risk was what it was all about. Farming was business, just on a different level.

Less risky items returned lesser rewards, but they were almost certain. Where you could really make your money was in the areas where you stood to lose the most if it failed, for any reason. I learned there were things I could control and things I could not, and I had to understand the difference if I was to make it to the next level. Minimizing risks and maximizing rewards was the name of the game. I was my own boss and my own slave driver. I just had to be smart and learn on the run.

• • •

My brother Stan came home from the Air Force in 1961—not a good time to be joining the workforce in the U.S. I remember one time when both he and his wife, Maureen, pooled their paychecks and realized that the two of them together had not been able to take home a hundred dollars. Times were tough.

I was a student at Orchard Lake out in Michigan at the time (Mom said I wanted to be a priest, though I had other ideas). To make money, I did things that have followed me throughout my life. I made Christmas wreaths, I sold whatever I could to make a buck, became what many people would call an entrepreneur, largely because I didn't give up. I didn't know any better. This is where I discovered calluses on my head from having been beaten so much with things that had gone wrong.

Stan was smart; he always found a way to make a little more out of our efforts so things were not as bad. Maybe he had learned something as an officer in the Air Force. I had more to look forward to than priesthood if I wanted it. We worked together and soon it became clear that if we wanted it to happen and were willing to work, this could become a going concern.

We formalized our agreement to go into business together in 1967, a "tenants-in-common" arrangement that served us both well in the years to come. Stan ran the business of Taft Farms, and I ran the farm end of things; together we both charted the direction we would take. For many years this proved to be the best workable model. Oh yeah, there were times we disagreed and almost came to blows, but we each respected the other's territory and somehow it all worked. We were more partners than brothers, but we got along and shared many a good time together.

The farm grew. At one time we were close to five hundred acres under cultivation between what we owned and what we rented. Those were the days when if you worked hard enough, you could still make a buck in this business; the idea of the big guy squeezing you out was still a long way off, though there were times we were stuck by someone who just couldn't seem to make ends meet. We dabbled in beef, veal, grain, corn, hay, just about anything that would make a buck. One year we harvested over fifty thousand bales of hay and three hundred tons of corn and sold it all!

Stan had that unique gift of being able to see a trend a long way off, long before it hit you, and make the decision to take action before you became overwhelmed. We entered into different schemes just in time to make a few bucks then left in time to save our skins. I still can't figure how he was able to do it. While other somewhat monolithic farms went out of business, Taft Farms grew and kept growing despite forces allied against it.

We attended every meeting offered, subscribed to every magazine out there, devoured all they had to say, digested it, and made our own decisions and somehow survived as a relatively small farm competing against giants. We built a new sales building and greenhouses, bought equipment, and expanded the business to the point it was profitable to support the both of us.

But it all came to a crashing halt when Stan's wife, Maureen, was diagnosed with cancer. She had been ignoring the symptoms, hoping they would go away, but they didn't. Through surgeries and treatments, she suffered for years. Tragically it ended, as it most often does. Maureen had been such a huge part of Stan's life that he became lost. All he had to return to at home was their dog, John; they had not had any children, and soon the toll became obvious on all of us. Absences became longer, tempers shorter. More of the administrative parts of the business began to fall on me.

One day Stan came into the farm and announced he was going on vacation. The reaction was mixed; were we glad he was finally going to get his head on straight? Or were we glad he was going away? Then one day he packed up a few things, strapped himself into his Piper Cherokee airplane, and started flying west. Those of us at the farm took care of John, his dog, and for nearly a year we heard nothing.

We got our answer when he returned almost eighteen months later. He had established himself a new life in St. Petersburg, Florida and wanted to sell off his part of the farm. From the moment Maureen had been pronounced terminal, I knew this day would come and had been quietly making assessments and plans but was still caught off guard. Under our agreement we each had the right of first refusal in the event of one of us selling out. Stan wanted to wrap the whole thing up rather quickly, but there was no way this could be accomplished in just a few months. Between appraisals, meetings with financial institutions and going to market in Boston, I was going nuts, not to mention I still had the farm and business to run, and Stan and I had yet to agree on a price.

Finally, the whole deal came together. Stan sold off and gave away things he chose not to take with him, packed the rest into his car and a trailer, and loaded up John. We shook hands and he was off.

In order to accomplish the buyout, I had to come up with a business plan that made sense not only to me but also my lenders, most of who had come to respect the way Stan had run things. It wasn't that the farm was in financial straits, because our footing was rather solid, it was the fact I had more than tripled its long-term debt overnight. We were no longer the kids on the corner with a fruit stand; we were an established business in the community with employees, taxes, and responsibilities. Keeping on top of everything and running the farm in its various forms gave me damned little time for anything else, and it began to take a toll on my family life.

My plan had begun with the obvious—what did I have to do in order to keep everyone happy? And then I worked backwards with the things and the quantity needed to generate that number. I found a few good people to work with and built a core, and for the first three years it all fell right into place, but then it happened: potatoes. More specifically, the Burbank Russet was a large part of the plan. Our farm soils were uniquely suited to the growing of this type of potato, and we grew some damn good ones. People came from all over, especially from ethnic groups living in Connecticut. Columbus Day weekend was one of the craziest times of the year and one of the most profitable.

But the Burbank Russet was a long-term, long-season proposition. We were on the borderline zone where they could be raised, and they required extra fertilizer and extra care. They had to be planted as early as possible and pampered to make the optimum yield. When things worked, we were golden because what we had in spades was market and our proximity to it. We also had IPM, something I'll get into later, and it was big.

What we didn't count on was Mother Nature. In the spring of that fourth year, things broke early, always a good sign. We were all planted with the potatoes by the first week in May, a full ten days earlier than ever before. Sweet corn was up, small vegetables were growing well, and plant sales from the greenhouses were going strong. Then we experienced more than six inches of rain over Memorial Day weekend. The Housatonic River could not stay within its banks and wiped out all our previous work. We had no choice. We had to start over.

We still had some seeds left, and I was able to get a few tons more at short notice. I had to juggle to get a short-term loan to cover fertilizer costs. Employees volunteered and stayed late but we got things in again. We did all we could, and then it was time to wait it out and keep tabs on things to make sure nothing else could go wrong.

The publicity generated by our pioneering of the new idea of IPM, Integrated Pest Management, had begun to show fruit from our labors. The basic idea behind IPM was that pesticides may be a part of your overall program, but they are not the primary focus. Everything from crop rotation to having the best understanding of the pests you are dealing with, to the use of mass quantities of natural predators, to any number of devices is used before one resorts to the use of chemicals. This sounds logical but technically can be illegal because we are not following label directions, but it works.

The season went well, perhaps a little more hectic and at times a little more hair-raising than we would have liked, but at least we functioned. Sweet corn was at least up to par, though not quite as early as we would have liked. Beans, an item we primarily shipped to Boston or other markets, were exceptional in quality, though the price was not what we expected; it was satisfactory but not what we needed. The potato harvest was lighter than we would have liked, but the quality was exceptional despite the late re-planting.

Then on the night of October 17, we had a freeze. Beets and carrots were destroyed, a loss we could tolerate under normal circumstances, but the pumpkins for Halloween were devastated. All the hay rides out to the pumpkin patch were off. We couldn't even find any to buy; the temperature had reached twelve degrees. Pumpkins everywhere were rotting in place.

Potatoes, underground though chilled, were still of acceptable quality, though storage was going to be limited. We kept digging, hoping for a strong market from the restaurants and the wholesalers handling our products. Eventually we finished the harvest. The celebratory bottle of Champagne was uncorked and disposed of, though the storage was less than half-full. It was all we could do other than hope for a higher-than-normal price in the winter.

By this time I had become pretty good at "robbing Peter to pay Paul," and I had a reasonable handle on how to make things work until the following spring, but there was one more arrow in devastation's quiver, and it was shot straight and true.

Strategy dictates you hit the holiday markets with whatever you have. It's when people spend their money and spare nothing to put the best on their tables. We had shipped as many baking potatoes as we could and only regretted not being able to ship more. The month of January is one of the toughest; it's cold, people get their credit card bills for the holidays, and they pull back and spend as little as they can. We try not to be in position to send anything then because winter doldrums tend to bring the lowest prices. If anyone wants to take time off, this is it. It's cold and we have to constantly monitor the temperature in the potato storage, though we are grading and packaging only once or twice a week. There is an alarm system to alert us if anything is not right.

I am a sucker. People tend to regard a farm as a place of last resort for employment on the planet, and sometimes I succumb. I had known Floyd Sr. since I was a kid. His son, Floyd Jr., was roughly the age of my oldest son, Keith, and they had known one another. This fellow had trouble with everything known to the modern world—drugs, alcohol, the law, you name it. I promised his father I would give him a chance, and everyone in the organization did, though he had occasional lapses. Junior came on board and started to look like he could turn himself around. Even in this tight season we all stuck with him and he appeared to make progress.

In January we all had to tighten our belts. Two or three days a week was all I could manage for anyone, even the single mother with three kids. We all just lived with it, knowing things would eventually get better. Junior had too much time on his hands. He got back into the drug and alcohol scene, maybe not as badly as before but bad enough.

On a bitterly cold night, a town nearby hit thirty below zero, someone opened the overhead doors of the potato storage, disabled the alarm system, and turned off the heat. It was an obvious act of vandalism. The local police could place Junior within a hundred yards of the storage unit when it happened but were unable to tie him directly to it, though the vandal had to have knowledge of the system he disabled and the ability to open all vents and openings. A regular person just off the street could not have done it. Though no court could ever find him guilty, a local policeman said I should seek "Silk stocking justice," a euphemism for revenge. I must confess, I thought about it and even told him in a private conversation what parts of his own anatomy he would be eating if he ever set foot on Taft Farms again.

Both his father and his mother passed away within a year. I think they both gave up. Junior never changed; he was hit and killed by a car after he staggered onto a busy street, drunk out of his mind, two years later. None of this changed my situation; I was in deep shit. I owed everyone, was months behind in all my bills, had no reserves, and was facing a new planting season with all its expenses. My insurance gave me a little money but any way I did the numbers they no longer worked. My situation within the community was no secret, nor did I intend it to be, but I needed help to survive.

It's often been said that when there's blood in the water the sharks come out. I had offers from a produce retailer who made a tantalizing offer on the farm but I killed it outright when he told me he would just bulldoze it to eliminate any kind of competition. I felt at least a bit of nostalgia and damned upset about a complete lack of respect. Stan and I had built this place with our own two hands. It meant something to me. If he was just going to demolish the place, couldn't he have waited until he owned it? Did he have to rub my face in failure?

Another offer came from a guy who claimed to represent a group that would turn our entire farm into a golf course. Not exactly what the town fathers had in mind when they designated us as the town's future water source since we were over a humongous aquifer. World-class was the word they used to describe the facility they intended to build. Arnold Palmer would be retained to design it. Wow! Just think how impressed the farmer must be.

Susan Witt and a few other local-minded individuals decided we were not yet dead. She put together a meeting of movers and shakers to see what could be done. Out of it came the idea of the state buying the development rights and the farm continuing to produce for local needs into the foreseeable future.

It all sounded too good to be true, and we eagerly signed on, though many of us came to regret the intrusion of the bureaucracy later. The state purchasing the development rights came rather quickly amid rather murky terms. The consequences were to come later when the answer to all my problems was to become evident and solutions more convoluted.

The attacks of 9/11 showed how vulnerable we Americans were. The result was an understanding that above ground water sources were not in the best public interest. Deep water, water that could not be contaminated, was desired, and Taft Farms was in possession of one of the best aquifers in the region, perhaps all of New England.

The Town of Great Barrington had known since the fifties that the geology under our farm favored the location of a major aquifer. I had even participated in a study conducted by one Ward Mott, after I assumed the full ownership of the land. Just after the attacks in September of 2001, the town's water people approached me about drilling a test well to see if there was water. Back in '93, when we started the process to put the land into APR (Agricultural Preservation Restriction), the town's selectmen eagerly signed on to the process, stating this was the best way to preserve the future water source for the people. Several town officials contributed cash, whether their intention was for that reason or not.

I had no reason to deny the attempt and took the liberty to consult with the hydro-geologist in charge of the project. He showed me underground maps, some of which were drawn by Ward Mott in his earlier study. The geologist explained that a narrow but strong vein of water roughly paralleled the river valley. He expected they would hit what they wanted, 1,000 gallons of water per minute, at about seven hundred feet. At 716 feet they found more than 1,200 gallons a minute. This guy was good.

The problem became the state. Despite the fact it stated black on white that the town was trying to preserve its future water source by entering our land into the preservation program and that town officials had contributed money to do so, and despite the town trying numerous times after to find water in other locations, the APR board decided they could not have it. I believe, after consulting with various individuals both at the state and local levels, that it was a pure case of jealousy on the part of the APR board. No matter what we or the town offered, they refused. Even when they at last told us what we had to do, and we did it, they refused, even though we met their criteria. It was as if they never expected us to comply with their demands, but we did. They did not dispute this fact but instead cited that they did not want to set a standard. In that way of thinking, a computer would serve the state better than a committee of bureaucrats and cost the taxpayers a lot less.

To this day the town has no deep water supply, though they know where it is. If anything were to contaminate the Green River, the town has less than two day's water supply on hand with no other place to get it and a committee of idiots in Boston that only know how to say no, mostly because they can.

• • •

Years passed. It was late 2017 and I got a call from the town's water company. They were having their monthly meeting and, believe it or not, the water from our farm was on the agenda. Surprise, surprise. Would I like to attend?

It was the Christmas season at the farm and I almost forgot about the meeting. Thank God Martha remembered. Quickly I gathered as much of the relevant information I could readily find and trotted into the meeting looking disheveled and late but at least interested in what they had to say.

The water company had spent millions drilling dry holes all over town and had found nothing of any interest. In short, there was only one place they had found what they needed, and they wanted to pursue that location... Our farm.

I recognized the man to my left at the table, Smitty Pignatelli, our state representative in Boston and was introduced to the fellow on my right, our state senator, Adam Hinds. The town was calling out the big guns. Both were chairmen of their committees on Beacon Hill and could cause moving and shaking to get things done.

The town had made a deliberate effort to comply with any reasonable attempt to find the desirable water source for the public, but turned up with *nada*, nothing, despite drilling in every location designated as a possible source within the town's boundaries, including the deepest well in the Commonwealth of Massachusetts. Little more than mud and iron bacteria were ever found. The only place with the water amount and quality was on our farm, and they intended to pursue tapping into this source one way or another. The water company had made as many attempts necessary to satisfy the Ag committee and had come up empty. The only way the town would be able to satisfy the needs of the community would be to tap into the resource available on our farm. Implied, of course, was that if an emergency occurred, the Ag committee might be held to account for dragging its feet.

Months passed. The commonwealth legalized marijuana for both medicinal and recreational purposes as well as its regulated growth. A farmer friend from a neighboring community decided to pursue a license to grow this new crop. He had years of experience from having done it outside the law, but he had a problem: His land was also in the APR program and APR land was expressly prohibited from this use.

He appealed to the board and they granted him approval.

I was unaware of this situation but a friend, a worker for the water company, was not and she was upset, to say the least. She called the chairman of the APR Committee in Boston and read him the riot act. The citizens of Great Barrington were being denied a secure water source, but those same citizens were going to get locally produced pot grown on APR land. Her next call was going to be to the governor. The one after that was going to be to *The Boston Globe*. What did the chairman have to say to that?

Our local water department and Taft Farms each received a call from the chairman. "Let's sit down and see if we can iron this thing out."

We've been talking but those talks are on hold. COVID-19 has made things more tenuous all around.

• • •

As of late 2020, much has happened to affect the farm. Two years ago I let my youngest son, Paul, now age forty, take over the day-to-day operation of the business, and by and large he's done a great job.

Martha and I like to think we had started something that would be continued for at least another generation or two. We've certainly worked hard and sacrificed things most would say we've earned. Our sons, Paul and hopefully Keith, and their wives will come to realize the value of what we have done. I would like to think that we have laid the groundwork for future generations to have a leg up on life, and that with some smarts and a little luck they will not have to go through the tribulations we have seen.

Though they have their own lives and I in no way wish to try to influence something I will never see, all I—as a father, grand-father, and hopefully great-grandfather—can hope for is they can appreciate the foundation that we have laid out for them. If they choose a different course, so be it. Whatever you may do, future generations, please do not forget those who have come before you and the sacrifices made to get you where you are. And please don't make the mistake of taking short-term gain for long-term loss.

Chicken Times

From the age of five I always had my designated chores. They weren't particularly difficult, but they were my job and they taught me a sense of responsibility and gave the satisfaction that you were, even in your small efforts, a part of the whole operation.

We always had chickens and, as the youngest child, my designated duty was to feed and water them and to collect the eggs. There always was a rooster or two with the hens. They acted as protectors, at least putting up a squawk when danger was near, and they often made life interesting for a small child. You always had to be on the lookout for the rooster. He would attack without warning, always from behind, leaving the unwary with scratches and bruises if he caught you unawares.

I was in my early teens when we finally gave up raising chickens. There just came a time when it was no longer economical. Large-scale producers, located almost anywhere else other than the harsh climate of New England, began flooding stores with cheap meat and eggs. At that point, I couldn't say I shed many tears over seeing the last of them go. Not only were they then a nuisance, but they had become costly.

Fast-forward about forty years. Taft Farms finds the potato business dried up, the bean market fallen apart and all we have is our retail store and relatively small acreage of vegetables that more than adequately supplies it. We need something else. Our retail has been growing at a substantial rate, but certain niche markets cry out. One of them is for fresh, all-natural chicken.

The news is full of stories about the inhumane treatment of animals, chickens in particular. Grossly unsanitary conditions on the farms and slaughterhouses, mass recalls of product, and illnesses traced directly to suspect chicken had swung public opinion against mass-produced meats. I remember one story that told of such horrible conditions it was only the survivors that were hauled off to the slaughterhouse. Small farmers producing a quality product begin to make a comeback. Price alone was no longer the principal factor in determining what people purchased.

I saw a notice about a seminar concerning small-scale poultry production for meat purposes and made a note. I was familiar with raising chickens. Yes, it had been years, but this might be just what the farm needed to bring in additional business. Pasture-raised chicken was not a new idea. When I was a child, our neighbors did it on a medium-sized scale only to find themselves squeezed out by mega-producers. This, however, was a little different. Instead of a large fenced-in yard, this system used smaller, movable pens that assured the birds of fresh grass and other greenery every day. Chickens are natural grazers. The fresh grass along with the grain we gave made for a naturally raised bird night and day better and healthier than the store-bought product. We jumped in with both feet.

The first batch of chickens was mostly given away as samples to show restaurants and other influential customers just what this product would look and taste like. The response was unanimous: We had a hit. Now we had to find a way to scale-up production to meet demand.

Raising chickens is not without problems, and soon these would come a-visiting. An unanticipated situation reared its head almost immediately. Many savvy consumers had been turned off commercial chicken because of the over-use of antibiotic medication. Our birds were therefore not inoculated, but that made them susceptible to just about any disease coming down the turnpike. We lost a lot of baby chicks until we discovered the way to keep them healthy was to add a small amount of bleach to their drinking water. I owe this bit of knowledge to a report I read from Penn State where some grad student had noted that chicken producers on municipal water systems had a lower incidence of disease than similar producers using well water. He attributed this to the very slight chlorination of many municipal water supplies. Ordinary household bleach at the minuscule rate of three ounces per hundred gallons proved sufficient to prevent diseases during those critical first three weeks in a baby chick's life.

One of the most amazing things about these baby chicks is the incredible speed at which they grow. They more than double in size every week. A one-ounce chick becomes a five- to six-pound chicken live, or a four-pound slaughtered bird, in about seven weeks. The modern meat bird, something called a Cornish-Cross, is an eating and growing machine. In fact, eating is one of their problems. If food is in front of them, they will eat it. They are capable of eating themselves to death. The grower must be careful not to feed them too much or he will kill them with kindness, especially if warmer temperature is expected. As the food digests it further adds to the normal heat the bird must dispel from its body. We tried everything we could but when all was said and done, the best thing was to be on top of the weather situation and cut back on the grain when warm conditions were expected. The fact chickens were out in the field on grass helped immensely, but we lost birds when temps reached the upper nineties. Their metabolism was such that there was no way to cool them sufficiently.

● ● ●

Over the course of the time we grew chickens, some notable individuals made their mark on the process. We at first started as a family operation. Together with my two sons, Keith and Paul, we were able to take care of the whole operation in the beginning but soon demand began to outstrip our abilities to fill it.

Pennie, our gal that basically ran the store, had fun selling the chicken to sometimes unsuspecting customers. All chicken was pre-ordered. We knew just how many to slaughter each week and Pennie knew who she could have fun with. One customer waited as Pennie ceremoniously brought forth her chicken. "Now this was Charlie. He was a good bird and you should treat him kindly, make sure you properly cook, and serve him. Treat his bones with respect as you lick them clean. He'd want that." I don't think too many people gave much thought to the chicken as ever having been a living being, much less having a name. Of course, this was all in fun but the looks on some people's faces were incredible. They had never thought of their food as having been alive. Pennie once told a friend that her title at the farm was "apprentice gizzard cleaner."

Sometimes you just get lucky. We were still in that stage where the three of us, with occasional help, were able to handle the slaughtering but one time it happened to be Senior Prom for Keith and Paul had an away baseball game. So there's Dad facing two hundred squawking chickens, all ordered, and no one to help. I was just about ready to start when Pennie told me there was a young man looking for a job out front in the store. Still in my apron and boots, I shook hands with a young but very tired-looking Black man with a heavy southern accent. I had an instant liking for this fellow and casually asked where he last worked.

"I worked for Perdue down in North Carolina until last week when I moved up here."

"Guess what, grab an apron. You've got a job."

Dave was a natural at this job; he'd been doing it for years. He could thoroughly clean and eviscerate a chicken, wash it, and get it in the ice tank in less than a minute. Together we finished the slaughter and thoroughly cleaned up in record time. He also said that compared to where he had come from, "You could eat off the floor here."

Since Dave had no vehicle, I offered to give him a ride to wherever he was staying. He seemed reluctant to accept my offer, but I convinced him it was no problem, and we left. His anxiety grew to the point I began to wonder if something was wrong as we moved farther away from the farm. Maybe he had no place to stay, but he assured me he was staying with his sister. We found her place and we shook hands as he left, greatly relieved. It all seemed so strange to me but the following day while we were out picking asparagus, he apologized for his behavior the day before. It seems that a Black man going for a ride with a white man down in North Carolina had maybe a fifty-fifty chance of being beaten, if not killed. That was the reason he was up here in Massachusetts. Someone was out to get him down there.

Dave stayed with me for that whole season. His sister and her kids became regular friends about the farm. It wasn't until the colder weather set in that he decided to move on to a friend who offered him work in Florida. We became quite close during the time he was here. More than one evening we killed a six-pack, solving the ills of the world. I heard from him a few times in the following years. He wanted me to come down so we could go fishing, as his job was on a charter boat. Sadly, we lost touch, but he left me with an insight to what it must be like to be a Black man in this country, especially in the South.

• • •

No completely normal person enjoys working in a slaughterhouse. We would all prefer not to have to kill anything, but it just needs to be done. Whenever a potential job applicant fills out an "app," I make a point of asking if they have a problem doing this kind of work. Some have said, "No thanks," and walked out.

One small blond-headed young man scared the hell out of me. He looked me right in the eyes and broke into the scariest smile I have ever seen. Licking his lips, he slowly whispered, "I just love to kill chickens."

No, we did not hire this fellow. I gave hard thought to calling the police. Maybe he had escaped from some mental institution or was thinking of running for president. None of us would have felt safe with him around.

• • •

As with any business endeavor, there are the good times and bad times. Predators can be a real problem. Every animal on this planet that eats meat eats chicken, or at least says that what they eat tastes like chicken. When small, chickens are vulnerable to almost any other animal, even those pests most regard as vegetarian. Other farmers have told me of even squirrels eating young chickens. Certainly, rats and even skunks must be considered predators.

Face it, chickens are stupid. Beyond stupid. I was having a predator problem and it was happening at night. I taped a flashlight to the barrel of a little .22 cal. rifle and went out searching for the culprit, and I found him, a skunk. But I couldn't get a good shot at him because he was pretty much covered with the juvenile chickens. You see, it was a cold night and the chickens were huddling up against the skunk to keep warm, lining up as the next to be eaten. I probably killed one or more of my chickens, but I got the skunk.

If a chicken escaped the pen, he was fair game for whatever came along. God only knows how many the foxes or coyotes got. It was not uncommon to see the trees around the field lined up with Red-Tailed Hawks or even Bald Eagles. One time I even stood by as an eagle tore apart and ate one of my chickens on a branch above my head.

The worst predator by far is the domestic dog. Huskies are the worst. I'm told they are only four generations removed from their wolf origins, and I've learned the hard way you just cannot trust them around chickens. A neighbor's husky killed more than two hundred of my chickens and then just wagged his tail at us like, "This is what I'm supposed to do."

Occasionally the predator is not one you would expect. One

morning, I went out to feed the chickens to find one pen torn up, and inside the pen was a Great Horned Owl. He had killed at least four chickens and had eaten the greater portion of one, terrorizing the rest, but could not find his way out. Horned Owls are an endangered species, so I carefully enclosed him in a burlap bag and brought him back to the store where one of my assistants brought him to a state forest many miles away before releasing him. I don't wish the owl any harm; I just want him to leave my chickens alone.

Raccoons are another problem. They are very deft with their hands, often reaching through a fine mesh screen to grab a chicken's leg and pull it through the screen. Then they proceed to calmly chew it off the chicken. Finding one-legged chickens in the pen does not make your day.

• • •

We almost religiously slaughtered between two and three hundred birds a week. This satisfied a few restaurants and our retail with maybe some left for walk-up customers. A mistake, actually a series of mistakes, led to an interesting season one year. Doug, the head chef at The Red Lion Inn had always purchased fifty to seventy-five birds for the barbeque on their patio. He would barbeque the breasts for guests and put the rest into a giant stockpot that cooked at low heat all day as stock for other soups. The night crew would take the stockpot off the stove before leaving, storing it in the cooler overnight. One morning, the morning crew tipped the stockpot over as they opened, but nothing came out. The stock had completely turned to gelatin. Doug said, "You've got something special here." His orders increased dramatically.

One day he gave me a call. "I know you need lead time so I'm going to tell you we are featuring your chicken for the fourth of July weekend, and we're booked solid, both hotel and restaurants. We're going to need at least two hundred of your chicken, maybe more."

Wow. I did the math and made my call to the hatchery where I purchased chicks, Hardy Brothers in Athol, Massachusetts. As it sounds, the business is run by two brothers, Frank and Bill Hardy. Bill took my call and turned to his brother, saying, "Taft just called and doubled their order." The next day, as Frank assembled orders, he came across ours, already doubled by his brother for eight hundred chicks. But wait, didn't they just double it? He sent sixteen hundred baby chicks. In other words, he doubled it again.

The next day I get a phone call from the Great Barrington Post Office asking me to please pick up my baby chicks. The racket was driving them nuts.

Now, what do you do with roughly four times the amount of baby chicks you usually order? It was going to be a tight squeeze with the original doubling but now it was twice as much again. We couldn't ship them back and we couldn't just throw them in the dumpster, so we grew them all. Space was tight and we did lose some as a result of overcrowding but then came Fourth of July weekend and Red Lion took closer to three hundred, and our regular and walk-up customers exceeded expectations, but we still had a lot of birds up to size and no orders. They continued to eat and grow at their unbelievable rate.

The next week, some of these birds dressed out at six to six-and-a-half pounds. This is the first time we ever got complaints that the birds were too large. "They're better than ever taste-wise but they're huge." What the hell do we do?

I made the executive decision to go back to our regular size birds and try to sell these "chickenzillas" piecemeal, as we got orders for larger size roasters. And they continued to grow. I never knew a chicken could get big enough to rival a turkey. Finally, at the end of the season, we slaughtered them all, and some were enormous. One chicken (emphasize *chicken*) weighed in at twenty-two pounds... dressed! In my wildest imaginings I never thought any chicken could get that large. It had to have been thirty pounds or more live weight.

We froze these chickens and stored them at a freezer plant

in Albany. When I finally went to pull them out of storage, the office refused to believe they were chickens. "These were turkeys—too large for chickens."

My family and staff at the farm ate a good many of these giant chickens, for we had a hard time selling them at this size, but anyone who tried one agreed these were the best chickens they had ever tasted. I still occasionally get someone asking if I have any more giant birds. Personally, I've never tasted a better chicken and I don't blame them for asking.

A side note: We've always allowed hunting on the farm, and the state even stocks pheasants as do private organizations. A hunter came up to me the autumn after the giant chicken episode, saying, "There's some giant white bird down there on your farm. It's too big to fly. What the hell is it?" Just after Christmas that year we found it, dead. An escapee, it had to have been at least thirty pounds. It was able to survive on its own until the really cold weather set in.

Finally, the decision was made to end our raising of chickens. They were good, the best I've ever tasted, but we were just trying to do too much. Something had to give, and it had to be the chickens. I still have a dozen or so laying hens at my house. I do appreciate the taste of a really good egg, but I miss the taste of real chicken, chicken to die for.

O Christmas Tree

Christmas is a major sales season at our farm. Its significance has grown dramatically over the years to the point it can no longer be ignored in overall planning. When I was still in school, it was little more than an excuse to drag in a few boughs, arrange them on wire coat hangers (they made a reasonable ten-inch wreath frame), and sell them to the patrons of my mother's hair salon for a few dollars. For a kid, this was just something to make cash used to purchase gifts for others.

As with other enterprises started by the young, if kept up, they have a habit of growing into something larger than ever thought possible. I just recently heard a pitch for a line of cookies going nationwide because a girl had started selling them "from her father's farm stand in the Hamptons." When you stick with something you believe in, even through the tough times, good things can happen.

When my brother and I left the teaching profession for good in the early seventies, the howls of just how crazy we were came from all sides. I say all sides, but both of our wives supported us to the nth degree. Though we both tried to find a workable scenario, it was understood there would be rough roads ahead. We had to maximize every opportunity and minimize each deficit just to survive. Possible, yes. Doable, not likely.

I have to give credit where credit is due: Stan was the reason we survived, along with a generous helping of just plain good luck. He was able to see an opportunity, ride it for all it was worth, and bail out just before it went sour. We worked like hell, around the clock more than once, caught a few hours of rest, and did it all over again. Exhausted most of the time, we still kept the operation going. The details are sometimes boring, tedious, and surprisingly redundant. Never was an idea that could bring in cash rejected, even something as minor as making a few wreaths and selling a few trees. This was how it started.

Over the years, more than I care to acknowledge, the Christmas enterprise has grown into a major part of the operation. From being largely just my effort, it has blossomed into the taking over of a major greenhouse for space to work, with a current employment of twenty-plus people, all of whom complain they need more help.

Every year the enterprise grows, sometimes a little, or like this year in 2019, by nearly fifty percent. I have no idea what was responsible for this dynamic growth. I would like to think it is a result of consistent quality or that maybe we are starting our ascent of the famous bell curve but no provable explanation has popped up just yet.

New people come aboard for the holiday rush, and each new face brings new sets of ideas to the table. A new design for greens, a new way to make bows... everyone contributes. By far the majority of new ideas have come from customers themselves, and sometimes from unlikely sources.

The colors were not what one could call traditional for the season, but a businesswoman, a Muslim by faith, put together combination bows that blew the senses away. She had a superb eye for beauty and freely shared her skills. Just referring to her decorations as "winter flourish," she taught us color combinations, non-traditional as they were, that got the point across for any faith wanting to celebrate the season. We've used her techniques for more than twenty years. She lives in Florida now, but I see her mother from time to time and thank her for raising a child with such exquisite taste.

The customers are the best source of stories, such as the man who showed me pictures of his cat, the cat who decided the best place to perch while watching the world go by was in the middle of the wreath hanging over the fireplace. Or the woman who had us makes a tiny six-inch wreath for her Dachshund to wear.

One of the most meticulous and demanding of our customers had to have been Jane Fitzpatrick, the owner and manager of The Red Lion Inn. She knew what she wanted and made sure she got it just so. Every year, even now after she has passed from the scene, we take special pains to make sure everything is exactly the way they want. There is a reason why The Red Lion Inn is held in such esteem.

• • •

Stories from the tree sales are hard to top from either sheer ridicule or fun. Just this past season the fellows selling the trees outside told of having to strap an eight-foot tree to the top of a Smart Car. Some years ago, I was faced with doing something similarly but to a Mazda Miata. A fellow with a Volkswagen Beetle convertible had to drive off with the top down, the tree sticking out the back in temperatures just above zero.

One of our more humorous tales was told by a man who claimed he lost a tree from the top of his car while returning to New Jersey. Somewhere on the Thruway, the tree flew off at high speed and crashed through the windshield of another car. Fortunately, no one was injured and all was properly taken care of, but the crazy part was the State Trooper investigating the accident. According to our customer (the tree in question had not come from us), the officer who filled out his report asked the party with the broken windshield, "Just how fast was that tree going when it hit your car?"

• • •

A competition of sorts develops between members of our male staff to be the one to sell trees. Christmas brings out the best of the customers and sometimes a little of the worst. I'm in my seventies now, and this year I was called out to help load the largest tree we had onto the top of a giant SUV. Kyle just could not do it alone, and after having had several shoulder surgeries I'm afraid I was probably not that much help, but we finally did succeed while three men, the purchasers—none more than forty—refused to help. They made sure to take plenty of photos but never even left Kyle a tip.

Tips are the reason my staff is so eager to sell trees. They go out of their way to ensure the customer is treated the best way they know how. At this time of year, it is not unusual for customers to throw a twenty into the tip jar. At the end of the day, the fellows can more than double their wages when they split what's been given.

There have been times when they earned every penny of it. One woman had our guys show her just about every tree we had. "Turn it this way. Let's look at this one." After more than two hours of tying up no less than two men she ended the session with, "I'm going to bring my husband. I can't make this decision myself." I don't know if she ever came back. If she did and the guys saw her first, I think they ran into the woods.

• • •

As our Christmas business has grown, each one of us has more or less found a specialty area in which to concentrate. Sue and Juan have become maniacs on two of the wreath machines. How many thousands of wreaths the two of them crank out is beyond me. To keep those two alone supplied with balsam prepared for whatever size they may be making at the moment can take four men armed with sharp clippers. As fast as the men can size material for Sue and Juan, they use it up. They make any size wreath from ten-inch rim to twenty-four-inch rim. A finished twenty-four actually measures more like thirty-six to forty inches, and each one is perfect. Occasionally, one of the cutters or another person fills in on a third machine if they have a large order. It is a misnomer of sorts to call these wreath machines. Actually, they are really wire wrapping machines, functioning only as a faster means of attaching the greens to the frame. The quality of the wreath is solely and strictly up to the operator. Sue and Juan are the best.

Antonio makes all the BIG STUFF. Anything larger than a two-foot rim is where he dwells. Size doesn't matter; he's made them as large as anyone has wanted. Occasionally, we have had to have rims custom-made for a customer, and Antonio has always come through, having to make them in as many as six sections to be assembled on site, sometimes with the help of a small crane. This year, Antonio teamed up with Juan to make three of the largest candy canes I've ever seen. It took four of us to carry each one out to the client's trailer. Though he didn't have one, he should have had a wide load permit. They were that big. How they managed to put them up on the side of a building I don't know, but the effect was stunning.

My forte is garland, or as we call it, roping. Ed and I make more garland than most can imagine. Garland, or roping, is made on a special high-strength twine. We have machines similar to those Sue and Juan use. The difference is that we wrap our greens on the twine rather than a frame. A bale of twine contains ten thousand feet. I used just about two bales, while Ed uses a little more than one. Any way you count it, that's about five miles of garland, mostly custom made to the specifications of the customer. We keep two and sometimes three cutters going as fast as they can.

One of the hardest things for a client to understand is why mixed garland costs so much more than garland made from a single kind of green, sometimes twice as much. From a strictly logical point of view I have to agree, until you take a look at where the rubber hits the road. Truth be told, the process of making garland becomes almost mechanical. The radio is playing and I can be talking to someone while still making the garland at the same rate. Throw in the idea of having to reach in a different direction for something with a strange consistency, make it fit into the overall picture, and you change the whole dynamic of the process. Add a third or a fourth component to the equation and everything changes. Your total concentration is required if you hope to turn out a quality product. Sometimes we turn the radio off and the "gatekeeper," Pennie, has to head them off at the pass. To produce a quality product, you must be able to concentrate totally on your work.

Ed and I both agree, it takes almost twice the time to produce the quality our clients demand when we add another item into the garland mix. The worst thing added is, without doubt, pine, ordinary White Pine. It is so sappy it drives us crazy. We have, however, found if not a solution, a partial answer: petroleum jelly. We are constantly coating our hands in the attempt to keep everything from sticking. It helps and makes washing up easier.

And then there are the other women: Racquelle, Sondra, Magalli, and a few others from time to time, who are responsible for the kissing balls for which we have become famous. I have always been harping on them about the time it takes to make each one, but there is no substitute for the quality. *No one* puts out kissing balls anywhere near the quality of the ones that come from Taft Farms, and these girls are responsible for all of it. High-end businesses from distances away call in for a decoration that is truly unique. Racquelle tries to train new hands but she is convinced only a few have the talent. There is no substitute for quality and she knows it.

As for the decorators, Sarah has been with us the longest, as was her mother and her grandmother. Creativity is not something that can be taught, only refined. IT is something that is either there or not. Sarah has it in spades, though she is constantly learning, refining, adapting to trends, even establishing new trends.

Sarah had four assistants this past season, each bringing a new approach to the same problem. They all learned from one another, and the result was spectacular. The sheer variety combined with the superb quality of decorated wreaths, table centerpieces, mantle pieces, and decorations of all kinds was almost beyond belief. Daily, sometimes several times a day, an enthusiastic customer came into the workshop clutching a newfound treasure. "Can I get four more just like this? I'm going back to the city tomorrow." We manage to take care of them all.

Trucks, Part I

Every truck seems to have its own personality. Some are referred to as "shop-trucks" because they seem to always be in the shop getting fixed. A friend who once worked as a road response mechanic told me he never saw a truck break down on the road, only at diners and rest areas. Drivers always managed to nurse them into a place where they could find food and entertainment while awaiting repairs.

It is said that at some time all things are delivered by truck. Merchandise can come from halfway around the world, but by the time it arrives—whether from a store, online or physical, or from a personal acquaintance—it has been in a truck, probably several times. Trucks are an integral part of our farm, as well. For our purposes, a vehicle does not have to be in the prime of its life. Almost none of those we've owned ever were. I can only recall us ever buying one brand new from a dealer. Inside of five years we ran this Chevy into the ground with over four hundred thousand very hard miles on it.

Most come to us through special deals, usually a former rental or lease for use on the road and from the junkyard for field use. Occasionally, when we have a special need, we'll hunt around to see what is out there. The pickup I'm driving right now cost me 700 dollars almost five years ago. Up till now, it has always passed inspection but I'm afraid it may be heading toward that great parking lot in the sky soon. The AC still works, a little less than I'd like, but body-rot has shifted into high gear.

• • •

One of the most memorable trucks we ever owned was a 1946 Studebaker one and a half-ton flatbed. I don't know where my brother Stan found this thing. It certainly didn't look like much, but it served us for two seasons. One thing for sure, it didn't owe us anything when it finally died; it only cost forty bucks and five bags of potatoes. But wow, did it smoke.

It always started, it always ran (Studebakers were tough) but it was just hard to have any long-term degree of confidence in something that cost so little, less than its junk value. We made many trips to Hadley, Massachusetts to pick up loads of potatoes and onions. Farms around Hadley grew large quantities of both, and we could double our money on each load. In many respects, this truck was responsible for the beginning of Taft Farms.

Each trip was an adventure. Nothing ever actually went wrong but the threat became increasingly hard to ignore, more than a quart of oil each trip. The turnpike was not an option. Break down on the toll-road and you really had a problem. We tested the weight capacity with each load, adding a few more bags each time. Actually, we bought as many as we were able to afford; times were tight.

On what was agreed to be our last trip of the year, we decided to have a little celebration. A twelve pack of Budweiser and a bucket of fried chicken would accompany us on this late Friday run, but first we had to get gas. Not a bad idea to check the oil either.

In those days, some kid pumped it for you and he even offered to check the oil. Sure, the old beast might need some, but it had stopped smoking, hadn't it?

"I got no reading on the dipstick." No wonder it had stopped smoking; there was no oil left.

"Put two quarts in," Stan yelled back.

"I still got no reading."

This was serious.

"Add two more," said Stan. It looked like this was going to be a fun trip home.

"You're still a quart low."

This was very serious. It only held five quarts to begin with.

"Okay, put it in. And hey, kid, can we get a couple gallons of drain-oil to take with us, you know, just in case?"

The back roads trip back west from the Northampton-Hadley area was not much longer in time than if one took the Turnpike. Any commuter working in that region knew this simple fact, but if the weather was bad it was easier to take the toll-road. It was sunny as we pulled out onto Massachusetts Route 66 just before four in the afternoon. Vehicles ahead of us soon disappeared but the line behind kept getting longer as the old Studebaker rumbled and chugged along. The good news, I guess you could call it that, was that the smoke had returned, with a vengeance. Every car behind us would need a wash. The car right behind even turned on his wipers—a big mistake.

The old truck had trouble making a respectable forty miles per hour, especially with the burden she was carrying, but at least the smoke had returned; that was a good sign, wasn't it? The beer and the fried chicken tasted good with no worries about disposal. There was no transmission cover (floor plate) between us, so the bones and cans could discreetly disappear right under the truck.

Occasionally, a car managed to pass, enduring the blue fog, bouncing beer cans, and chicken bones. In my mirror I saw the first car had his wipers on, but the driver had his head out the window. His windshield was one big smear.

Then came the hills and sharp curves. From our almost re-spectable forty we dropped to thirty... downshift... to twenty... downshift. But still our speed dropped, and we were finally in "grandma," but at least we were still rolling... and belching. Having to go this slow just meant more chicken, and of course more beer. Route 66 was too narrow and winding for anyone to pass, and an occasional honking caused us to give a glance in our cracked mirrors. The happy motorists were getting restless;

with no way to pass, they just had to endure. Well, at least the top of the first hill was in sight. Two more beer cans and some chicken bones went down through the floor, some napkins, too, I think.

At last, the RPMs rose, and Stan shifted up. A car pulled out, assessing whether he could pass, but someone was coming the other way. He ducked back in, wipers still smearing oil, his washer fluid long since exhausted. By now we were doing our respectable forty miles an hour again and another curve and hill were coming up. It was time for more chicken bones as we started the downshift. Soon we were crawling and belching along again in first gear. I opened another can for Stan and one for myself. There seemed to be more than one horn joining the chorus behind us, but what could we do? No place to pull off, no way to speed up, no way to stop the smoke. To hell with them if they couldn't take a joke. Only a half dozen more steep hills and about twenty more sharp curves remained before we came to Route 112 in Huntington. They were just going to have to endure it. That was the first place we had any hope of pulling off to let them pass; by then we would have to check our oil anyway. We had another beer and some chicken, bones and empties. Not a problem.

The horns got louder; a lot louder—not many friends behind us. Finally, there came a short straightaway and the guy with the wipers pulled out. He pulled alongside and put down the passenger side window.

"I'm calling Runsdorf Trucking, and you guys will be fired."

Stan and I looked at one another, then realized the name of the company that had owned the truck, probably several owners ago, was still on the doors. No one had ever removed it. Stan held a can of beer up to the guy as he sped away, nearly losing it on the next curve. "To Hell with him."

We finally reached the stop sign where we merged with Route 112. I don't know if anyone behind us noticed the difference in speed. At least this was a little more level, but the curves remained until we joined US20. Finally, there was a place to pull off and check the oil. The gas was okay. It was the oil we were worried about.

The old Studebaker needed almost four more quarts, but we had it with us. At least fifty cars passed us, many blowing their horns, displaying the famous one-finger salute. We were not the most popular guys that day. More than one motorist needed a carwash, and some may have been late for appointments, not that we could have done anything about it.

The '46 Studebaker made it home, the chicken and beer long since consumed, and actually continued to serve us for another year. Finally, it was running on only one, maybe two of its eight cylinders, using more oil than gas, and eventually it went to that Great Parking Lot in the Sky.

• • •

We've had a few memorable vehicles at the farm. The Studebaker was perhaps one of the most important because it was one of the ones that got us up on our feet but the one that finally put us over the top had to be the '62 Chevy.

Purchased used from a dealer it represented a big step for our fledgling organization. The Green Chevy had been formerly owned by a man who used to collect cannons. That's right, cannons. Because he traveled a lot and took his cannons with him to various celebrations, the truck had extra-heavy springs on it. The only reason he sold it was because he bought a bigger cannon.

Officially, this truck was also rated at a ton and a half, just like the Studebaker, but with all the additional springs and over-sized rubber, we were able to use it to haul just about all the weight we could put on it. Whether nursery stock, equipment, grain, fertilizer, or just about anything else, the Chevy could handle it.

I personally put a lot of miles on it, traveling all over the Northeast. It didn't have a functioning radio but had one of them "new-fangled" eight-track stereo tape decks. I only had a dozen or so tapes and had each thoroughly memorized by the time I graduated into something a little larger with a functioning radio.

I never had a breakdown with that truck, taking it as far away as southern New Jersey and Ohio, but it was not always the most comfortable way to get there. Finally, after we bought a larger truck for over-the-road hauling, the Chevy was converted into a potato truck during the harvest season. It served us well for years before it finally went for scrap just this past spring. We hadn't run it for a few years. Rust and age claimed another.

• • •

A local junkyard has kept us supplied with "runners" to work around the farm. Most were deemed too expensive to fix for road use but still had some life left in them, usually in the form of a pickup or van. Several of our younger workers learned how to drive with these limited-use trucks.

One old Ford I recognized as having come from a nearby ski area. It was about as badly beat upon as any vehicle I've ever encountered, but it still ran and did its job for more than a season. I recognized it because the kids at the ski area had taken the Ford name from the hood of the truck and reversed the "D" and the "F" so the truck became a "DORF."

It's next to impossible to get up any kind of speed on the farm roads. That's a good thing because it was not that unusual to have large pieces and parts fall off these wrecks. Perhaps one of the craziest things I ever personally saw happened when a pickup literally broke in half. One of my Latino workers hit a bump just after entering our parking lot, and the truck split apart right behind the cab. He had it in four-wheel drive at the time, and although the bed stayed behind, he continued to try to drive the front half even though he had to look out the window to see where he was going because he was nearly sitting on the ground.

He didn't get very far. He ran out of gas, as the tank was in the rear part of the truck. I later found out from one of his friends that he was afraid I was going to fire him because he had broken one of my trucks, literally. We all had a good laugh. Our friends at the junkyard were already on the way to retrieve the wreck. In two pieces.

• • •

Susie, our flower person, has appropriated one of the vans for her use, and her use only. She needs to have a covered space as well as lots of room for buckets of cut flowers. She is amazing for the sheer quantity of flowers she grows. At one point she had nearly six acres of flowers for cutting, and they were gorgeous.

Sue carries everything she needs in her van, or as she puts it, "My whole life is in there." Sometimes as many as three arrangers are kept busy with the loads of flowers she brings in from the fields. On summer weekends, hundreds of retail bunches as well as those cut for wholesale decorators, weddings, parties hosted by the region's glitterati, and "too numerous to mention" restaurants pass through the farm. And almost all of them pass through Susie's hands and ride in her Flower Power van, which sometimes doubles as a hay wagon when she's feeding the animals.

Amazing Corn

Public fascination for simple entertainment never ceases to amaze us farm folk. Cut-outs of cartoon characters, animals, even vegetables, that a child can stick his face through for a photo are so popular we have trouble coming up with them fast enough. Animals, not the exotic kind, but those expected to be found on a farm (even if only from a children's book) draw kids in quantities none of us ever thought possible. Of course, the kids bring at least one adult for the ride. Often they bring extended family—grandparents, aunts, uncles, and neighbors. When this happens, having critters starts to make sense. Adults bring wallets, and children open those wallets. But it's the corn maze that attracts the most attention during an all-too-brief, six- to eight-week season. Often several hundred people will try to find their way through each day just to say they did it.

If the corn is thick and tall and the number of choices appears endless, adults find the task challenging. Kids run around, burn off energy, and thoroughly embarrass parents by finding the proper route. From the outside one can hear the conversation. Excited children running every which way, having fun while parents, and sometimes grandparents, debate whether or not they have taken this path before, "No, we should go this way. We've already taken that trail. It's a dead end." Bottom line: kids love it, Mom and Dad get frustrated.

The idea of a corn maze was something toyed with for years, but it wasn't a solid selling point until I had a conversation with a farmer friend from the Albany area. He had started doing a maze five years ago and seen an interest grow by leaps and bounds. He expected over 50,000 visitors to his farm just because of his maze. This number grabbed my attention. Even after allowing that he was located near a much larger population center, this was a number to which any retail establishment would pay attention. Downtown stores, mall stores would give eye and tooth to attract those numbers in a six- to eight-week period. He encouraged me to give it a try. I was far enough away to have no effect on what he was doing, and my primary customers were the weekenders coming from Boston or New York while his were locals from the Albany area. He offered any assistance needed.

The idea of a corn maze meant we would have to sacrifice the use of prime growing space near the store. You cannot expect people to walk any distance to get to this attraction. It was hard to factor into the general farm equation. For as long as the farm had been in existence, we had always planted what we referred to as smaller veggies as close to the store as possible because they had to be harvested sometimes on a moment's notice. You couldn't plant parsley in the field across the river if you had to pick it four or five times a day. Difficult changes were needed. Cut flowers—an item whose demand was growing like "Topsy"—had to be moved. Even tomatoes, another crop that sold itself based on visual impact, had to find a home farther afield.

There may have been bruised egos among the staff, but all was healed when the response became obvious. Adjustments were necessary, and within two years all was well again on the farm. All managers, nominally in charge of a particular area, realized the value the corn maze held for the public. We were selling more of everything because more people were coming. Kicking and screaming we were drawn into the world of entertainment farming.

Our first maze came in the beginning of the Star Wars phenomenon. Though I had experience in making large, oversized banners, I had few ideas concerning what we were about to attempt. The concept is relatively quite simple: find a picture of what you want to project and cut it into equal grids, squares. Take flags or markers of some sort or another and mark out the field into the same number of squares in roughly the same configuration. You then carve out the walkways by transferring the big picture square by square. Theoretically this works, but doubts remain until you see it from the air.

Our first attempt was a caricature of Darth Vader's helmet, a popular image. Making a caricature was not that difficult, but I agonized over the field grid. Was it measured correctly? Would it fit on the field planted? I had to go with the best instinct I had, and I cut the corn accordingly. Had I just made the biggest mistake in the history of Taft Farms? I measured twice and cut once, as the rules said, but would it look anything like Darth Vader's helmet?

A former employee, a flight instructor at the Great Barrington Airport, offered to take me up for a look. Sue, my greenhouse manager, went along to provide moral support. She warned me she always got airsick. If she upchucked it wasn't because she didn't approve. As we banked over the farm, the most prominent image was that of Darth Vader snarling back at us. I was beyond elated. What I thought might work actually had beyond my wildest expectations.

After we landed, Tom told me he had been flying sightseeing tours out over the maze as soon as he noticed it. Did we mind? Are you kidding me? Pictures of Darth Vader in corn showed up in local newspapers. People wanted to know how I had done it. Did I use G.P.S. or some other form of pinpoint navigation? I answered every question, told them all how simple it really was, but most refused to believe it. Some even insisted I must have had help from E.T. Just like they must have had on the plains of Nazca in Peru. The maze was a hit. With the news coverage, families came from everywhere and business at the farm store was never better.

Armed with a little self-confidence, I decided to aim for greater heights the next season. The challenge was to come up with themes to attract kids. Attracting children was key to the effort. Kids can be relentless. Eventually, Mom and Dad or grandparents will give in, especially if it's for free. Getting people in the door, that's what it's all about. We also decided to go big, maybe have more than one maze.

There is no such thing as a generic child; siblings can be as different as night and day, but we knew we had to come up with at least three different mazes to satisfy the age groups. For the little ones we grew shorter corn and cut a simple rising sun with a few cartoon cut outs, places for them to put their faces for a photo. For those a little older we had two mazes. This was about the time the Harry Potter books broke onto the scene. I managed to make a smiling Harry, complete with eyeglasses and unruly mop of hair. This took up almost four acres and came out better than expected. Pennie Curry, our store manager, had a dozen very authentic signs made up for Hogwarts, Diagon Alley, and such. The maze was difficult but not bad, and the signs and other props made by Sue Hayden, the greenhouse manager, gave it a real professional look.

The next maze was more difficult. I did a straight-on face of Aslan, the lion from Narnia. The face part was not that difficult … it was his mane. I designed and cut the thing and still I became lost more than once. All the routes looked the same. After a few signs and props, Aslan was ready to take on the world.

These three mazes had taken more than a month. On occasion during construction, I had noticed private aircraft circling overhead. The word was out. I decided to make it even more obvious by simply cutting a large "Welcome to Taft Farms" along the edge of the field containing the two "master" mazes. It wasn't difficult, space adequate. I was still putting my tools in the truck when a small plane came overhead wagging its wings. I waved back. I was on top of the world. But … pride comes before the fall.

Labor Day Weekend we were scheduled to open the mazes. Other than a couple small ads placed in local flyers and posters, no formal advertising was done in advance. An aerial photo appeared in *The Berkshire Eagle*. Someone posted a photo on Facebook taken from enough height that all the mazes and even the "Welcome" showed up clearly. Oh, boy... get ready for this one!

Saturday morning and cars started to arrive. I lost count but several hundred showed up and the feedback was all positive. They loved it. The weather forecast indicated a possibility of severe thunderstorms that evening, and right on cue clouds started building in the northwest. Before five I closed the mazes just to make sure everyone was out, but the storm took its time to build to full strength. Just after dark it hit, and it was ferocious. There was nothing I could do but wait for daylight and fix what needed to be fixed before maze-goers arrived.

When I pulled in the next morning, the first thing I noticed was my neighbor removing what was left of his retractable awning from his house. His wife was attempting to retrieve lawn furniture and other debris from the small swamp a hundred yards from their house. Then I saw my mazes ... completely flattened. Not one stalk of corn remained standing in nearly ten acres. Even the small children's maze was destroyed.

Bob and Diane, our neighbors, walked over to where I was standing dumbstruck. Bob said they were having dinner when the storm hit. The wind kept increasing and then they heard what sounded like a freight train. They ran into the basement and clung to each other for dear life. They heard glass smashing but fortunately it was only a lawn chair coming through their patio door. The local radio station assured me there had not been a tornado, but an intense microburst had indeed touched down. Other than the corn mazes, and bruised feelings, we had no physical damage. We never even lost power.

Again, I lost count of the cars and people coming for the maze, but now they were turning away, disappointed. What could I have done differently?

I was more than a little soured by the idea of making a maze, also humbled to find that no matter how well made it could disappear in a matter of minutes. I was ready to call the whole thing off and not do any more. A corn maze is not that challenging, but it is a lot of work, hard work, by any number of individuals, most of whom never receive the appreciation they deserve. Most of the credit (in this case, blame) is heaped on me but someone like Sue, a frustrated thespian, I'm sure, rarely receives the adulation she deserves.

I was tending toward the negative, but Pennie and Sue convinced me to give the whole thing another try the next season. Emotionally, I had poured myself into the project and the level of quality achieved surprised us all. To have the whole thing wiped out after only one day of operation was more than I wanted. I'd endured other disasters, both natural and man-made, but this one had cut to the quick. My soul had wanted this one to succeed. I think it was the enthusiasm shown by others in the face of disaster that convinced me to try one more time. Both Sue and Pennie had invested time and energy, but somehow neither of them seemed deterred. Despite my showing them both how simple it was to set up the maze (far more difficult to cut) they both insisted they were unable to put it together. They had a continuing case of the same doubts I had years earlier. I couldn't blame them. I was trapped.

We moved the maze to a smaller field closer to the store, in fact, the same one where Darth Vader had made his appearance. The chosen image was Shrek and Donkey. The result was a resounding success. Again, aerial photo confirmed everything worked as planned. Customers flocked to the store and on some weekends, traffic caused minor problems. Children brought adults, who brought their wallets. Thank God. Winters are long here in the Berkshires.

The very idea of a maze and entertainment became what people expected from Taft Farms each autumn. Local musicians performed at the store wowing out-of-towners with talent few expected this far from the city, as if New York was the only place anyone could expect to find gifted performers. One group in particular, a family, impressed like no other. The father played guitar but was in no way the lead. His seven-year-old daughter played the drums while her eleven-year-old sister played the most amazing violin-fiddle you have ever heard. The cash in the violin case was astounding. One appreciative listener tossed a 100-dollar bill in the case. WOW. I want those people back, especially the performers.

Occasionally, our mazes are not in the shape of something but rather a run through, based on a particular idea. We've also carried this into a haunted theme. One of our most successful displays (it would be hard to call this one a maze) was a walk-through with lifelike and almost life-size dinosaurs. What kid doesn't like dinosaurs? Other displays featured cutouts of superheroes, and another time, favorite cartoon characters. On a Lords of the Jungle theme one year, we featured the maze cut to be a giant crocodile while side paths led to life-size rhinos, elephants, lions, etc. Kids eat that up.

We're always open to suggestions and they usually come from the kids themselves. Whatever is hot in children's literature or the movies wins out, even if I've never heard of it. This past year an animal series based on polar bears, husky sled dogs, and domestic cats came to the fore. It was called "Hunters, Seekers, Warriors." I'm still not sure which animal represented which topic, but it looked good and the kids loved it.

If kids want it and they keep bringing Mom and Dad, we'll keep making them. My part, the cutting of the corn, is rather simple, just so long as I don't let the corn get too high. The whole thing is based on visibility. The easiest way to make a corn maze is to have a picture of what you would like to cut, one of outlines with as few shadows as possible. Here is where cartoon characters make the process easier. They are often flat and one-dimensional. Subtleties are hard to bring across in something as regular as a field of corn. We try to reduce the picture to lines only—outlines, facial features and major characteristics are about all you can expect to do, unless you have a large field with many acres. I've seen some truly incredible and lifelike images, but they are done in fields much larger than I'm willing to dedicate for non-crop use.

Once you have a satisfactory image, one that is doable in the space you've allotted, convert it onto a standard piece of paper, eight and a half by eleven inches, and draw lines both vertically and horizontally to cut it into a grid. I try not to exceed a ten-by-ten grid. Keep it as simple as possible. Too many squares will make the job a lot harder than it needs to be.

I have a four-row corn planter. After I, as accurately as possible, plant the rows one way, I plant them the other way, exactly square, ninety degrees from the first set. This makes the layout much easier; ten rows by ten rows equals a square. Remember, I'm not planting this to make a crop. Good weed-control is a necessity. The next part is probably the most time consuming and difficult. You must accurately mark off the field into the same number and pattern of squares. Depending on how tall the corn has become this can be simple or hard enough to make you curse... loudly. I try not to let the corn get more than three feet high before I mark off the squares, and I use five-foot stakes with surveyor's fluorescent tape tied to the top as markers. Corn grows fast in the summer. By the time I have finished marking out and cutting the maze I have trouble finding the stakes, even with the bright tape tied to the top. With a clipboard in one hand and a sharp machete in the other, I transfer the design from a single square on the paper to the corresponding square in the corn. It's easy if you can see your way around. Once the corn gets up above the stakes it can be hell. I try to make a quick rough-cut as fast as possible, at least make trails I can follow, and finish this cut before the corn gets above the stakes. If I have three-foot corn to start, I count on it becoming stake-high in a little over a week, so I've got to work fast. But I'm not home free the moment I finish the first cut. As mentioned before, corn grows fast, and can grow back fast, even when chopped down. It puts out what are called tillers or side-shoots, especially when the process is triggered by cutting off the main stem. In little more than a week the tiller growth can make it difficult to find where you have cut your trails. I have become lost in places I cut only a short time before. I've had to look for cut corn on the ground rather than rely on where I think I went. The second time through makes the most difference but some regrowth occurs even after this harder cut. Often I go through the trails with my lawn tractor to remove any corn stumps that remain. I also try to remove all the marker stakes while I can still see them.

Corn leaves are sharp, as anyone who has ever picked it on a hot day can tell you. As it brushes past tender skin it can not only raise a welt but can even draw blood. Just before opening I go through one more time, slicing off leaves and tillers that have grown out from the side of the trails. This is to minimize the risk to anyone who decides to run and have the leaves rub along their neck. It really can hurt.

Now, this is only what I do. During this time, Sue and others have already been working on props and signs for weeks. All their work must be carried into the maze and set up, assembled in place. How about dragging in a nearly full-size T-Rex. Some assembly required. Oh, and you can't knock over the corn. Despite all the headaches, when you see the smiles and hear the comments, it's worth it, and we'll do it again next year.

In the age of the coronavirus pandemic, we were forced to limit the number of people allowed in at one time. Our theme for 2020 was a "Tribute to the First Responders." The maze was a highly stylized Peace Dove.

Kiss and Tell

It's been twenty-five years or more since the handsome guy with the Bentley made an appearance in the store. Athletic, well groomed, and obviously wealthy he caused a stir with the younger, eligible female members of the staff. Since we never saw any companions, speculation abounded. "Was this guy for real? What the hell was he doing here in Great Barrington?"

He was maybe forty at best, with no hint of a spouse, no ring, no nothing. Maybe this guy was eligible. "Wow, what a catch he would be."

I could not help but notice how the women at the farm (and some were quite attractive), suddenly became even more perky, responsive, and attentive to their appearance. Hair was done better, colored, and styled. Clothes were chosen with greater care, coordination paid attention to, and some worked on cleavage not usually seen in a fruit market setting.

When James (I never did get his last name) showed up, there would be a rush for the lady's room and the mirror. "Is my lipstick too bold?" "I wish I could get this shine off my nose." "I washed my hair last night and I can't do a thing with it." I think I heard every conceivable female worry wart phrase in existence, but to no avail. "Handsome James" only wanted to talk to me. He never made any gesture, overt or otherwise, but had to be aware of the arousal he caused. Several times he commented about Lynn's willingness to get "whatever he might desire" or Kathleen's smile that could melt an iceberg. This guy could have any woman he wanted. To a female he was the catch of the century, but in reality no one was going to own him. He was his own man, one who moved in very exclusive circles. We both smiled, enjoying the theater. He was a likable guy; someone you could have a beer with and shoot the breeze.

As soon as we started picking sweet corn, he came nearly every day. He was an addict of sorts. The plates on the Bentley indicated he came from Texas, most probably in town for something to do with the arts scene, perhaps a patron. He must have had sweet corn before but ours seemed to have made an impression because he kept coming back daily, as if he couldn't help himself.

I never found out whether James was married, attached, or otherwise latched onto but he took merciless glee in torturing the staff side of the aisle. He had a Hollywood sort of attraction to him, and if he smiled at one of the girls she was in heaven while the others all hated her. He was an overall good sort of guy and never led anyone on, though he certainly could have, and he came nearly every day, but always alone.

It was easy to see this fellow operated on a different level than the greater portion of society, even if one only noticed the car that had to have cost at least a quarter of a million dollars. He never dressed exceptionally, once coming in wearing a Mickey Mouse tee shirt, but there seemed a purpose to his demeanor, a command to his presence, that let all know he was not to be messed with. He had major connections but never any companions....

One day, he approached me with a proposition. He wanted to ship some of our corn to a friend overseas. He would arrange for everything; all we had to do was supply the product. That would be easy enough, but there was one stipulation. He wanted to say he picked it himself.

"No problem," I answered. "Just get here early when we start picking and let me know a day ahead of time."

The appointed day arrived. The girls came in early, for there were things that needed to be done. Funny, they'd never shown such attention to detail before; everything was perfect, especially their appearance.

James and I jumped into my pickup and headed out to the cornfield. He was thrilled, but we had to leave several female volunteer pickers behind. The morning mist was still in the air and this was a whole new experience, something he would remember. His smile was genuine, adventure at hand. Other than birds, most of the world was not yet awake—no planes overhead, no traffic, the only sounds coming from wildlife and the cicadas.

I took the opportunity to ask what he did for a living.

"Oh, I'm in petroleum."

"Do you own a chain of gas stations or something?"

"No, petroleum before it becomes gasoline. I'm in exploration and development. I even do off-shore drilling."

Now I knew where the Bentley came from. The cost of gas was incidental, maybe even a write-off. I never figured this man was worried about his next meal, but he could have fed a small city.

We picked a couple dozen ears, each perfect, and headed back to the store. We both munched on a raw ear. I did this all the time but for him it was new, another first. His smile told the tale—he was no different than the rest of us.

From the trunk of the Bentley (I think they call it a boot), he produced a special Styrofoam box designed for shipping, one of those "Space-Age" containers featuring ultra-insulating material weighing next to nothing. We carefully husked, down to perhaps only one green layer, each ear before placing it as precisely and compactly as possible into what appeared to be something designed especially for this purpose.

A stranger had appeared, unnoticed, with a camera, documenting the proceedings. The whole procedure took on a life of its own, even more so when Lynn informed us a limousine was waiting in the parking lot.

"Thank you," answered James, smiling and checking his Rolex, "He's right on time."

Just what the hell was going on? This whole thing was bizarre.

Paul Abbott from Abbott's Limousine Service was waiting in the parking lot with a stretch-job. James ceremoniously handed him the special box and reminded him it had to be on the ten o'clock flight to London. The necessary labels were waiting at the British Air desk. James paid me for the corn and a little extra, for special consideration, and Paul Abbott was off to the airport with the photographer.

"Aren't you at least a little concerned with customs or plant inspection people?" I asked.

"No, it's already been taken care of. They won't even give it a look; they know where it's going. Besides, it will arrive on the Concorde." He smiled with the confidence that I knew what he meant. Supersonic Sweet Corn. This was important stuff.

This guy had all the connections but what he had just done must have cost more than I make in a month, maybe several. A great deal of money was being spent to ensure that very important people got to taste very special, sweet corn.

A week's time passed, and James had become conspicuous by his absence. I was beginning to wonder if there had been something wrong with the corn. Then he showed up on Saturday morning but didn't look quite himself. "You've probably seen the papers," he said. "The whole thing's gone crazy."

I had no idea what he was talking about. In our season we let only two things bother us, growing the product and selling it. Things were going well at that point.

He held up a copy of the *Sun* of London, a Rupert Murdoch rag sheet, with a front-page picture of Princess Sarah Ferguson, Fergie as she was known to most, cavorting topless on some island in the Mediterranean with a man other than her husband. Her two children were playing nearby. The grainy picture had been shot from a great distance but there was no mistaking the principal characters.

I may not have been totally in touch with the times, but I had heard of the affair, for it was almost impossible not to. The male in the picture was her "financial advisor" and the stories coming out of her unhappy marriage were the start of legend.

"I sent the corn to her friend, a friend of mine," James advised. "He's also my financial advisor. They had it on their dinner table just before they left on this ill-fated trip. I hope they enjoyed it. They are good people and deserve better. Her husband is a total boor."

I never saw James again. He might have come in, but no one ever said anything about it. The girls lapsed into their normal appearances and the farm remained a farm, no royal connections, let alone subsidies. Fergie and her husband separated. I don't know what became of the "financial advisor."

Looking back through records one day I almost did a backflip. The corn we had picked for shipment to Fergie and friend was from Johnny's Selected Seeds in Albion, Maine, and the variety was named Kiss and Tell.

How prophetic could anything be from this side of the pond? I'm not making this up, folks. I couldn't have done that in a million years if I tried, and it's damn good corn.

Mendel Squash

I've always been a proponent of seed saving, not of the everyday ordinary item readily available from any reputable seed house, but the unusual, the one plant that just seems to show up with a significant difference from the rest of the crop. Over more than six decades I've been growing, strange items have made their appearance in my gardens. I wish I had saved seeds from them all but I did not. What untold treasures passed me by I'll never know, like the very tasty cherry tomato with thorns. A few that piqued my curiosity I did save, and these in turn may someday save our farm.

Back in the sixties, our main crops were potatoes, corn, beans, and pumpkins and squash, probably in that order of importance as well. Finding an unusual potato plant would be a stretch of the imagination since they are seldom grown from seed in the traditional sense. Potatoes harvested from the previous year are planted to produce the new crop. Not much hope here in finding that "as yet" undiscovered variety. Cross-pollination rarely occurs in the field and is difficult even in the lab. Potato variety development is best left to those in the laboratories.

Corn types are also best left up to the researchers, though there can be exceptions. More on this later because the Native Americans seemed to have had a pretty good idea about seed saving. Literally thousands of varieties of sweet corn and probably just as many of grain corn are commercially available to the grower, and most are good to excellent in quality.

Back in the late sixties we had a serious drought. Whatever it was, if you couldn't get water on it (irrigation) you had a problem. Our farm was mostly on low land, so it was not as bad for us as others, but we had planted our pumpkins on the gravelly upland and they were suffering.

Autumn came along with the harvest. The pumpkins were small. Sugar, or "pie" pumpkins, normally three to five pounds, were at best one pound. Most field pumpkins (your jack o' lantern type) came in at about five or six pounds. Truly this was a disaster, but there was one plant in the middle of the worst drought affected area that said "No." This truly special plant had one pumpkin weighing over sixty pounds and at least five more between thirty and fifty pounds, and each was absolutely perfect in shape and quality. If you were going to save the seed from any plant, this was it.

We only saved the seed from the largest one, and the following year (also a year of low rainfall) it thrived. While other growers reported crop failures, we had one of our most successful pumpkin crops ever. By the way, the seed we purchased failed to live up to catalog expectations but the pumpkins from our own seed were spectacular.

We knew we had something, but what? Our strain was at least drought-resistant and was larger than the norm, but what else did we have? Over the forty-plus years since we first identified the particular strain we wished to pursue, we have identified drought resistance, size and shape, unbelievable growth vigor, and resistance to many of the common diseases. It has also developed a stem that's hard to break off under normal conditions. Any commercial grower will tell you that this last attribute is one of the most desired traits you can have.

About fifteen years ago, a representative from a major seed house convinced me I should try to market this new kind of pumpkin. I bit on the bait but something in the back of my mind said I should be careful, so I didn't send him what I considered my best seed but nonetheless good stock. "Oh, we had a crop failure, but from what we saw it doesn't look like anything we can use."

Now, I might not be the brightest light in the universe, but I could sense a scam. Two years later his company came out with, "A revolutionary breakthrough in pumpkins." You can guess what some of the most important traits were. Their "very special new pumpkins" were virtually identical to what I had sent him. I knew I'd been had but other than signed receipts that he had actually received the seed, I had no case, my lawyer assured me. I learned, but I still had better seed, another card to play. "Jamie," if you ever get to read this, you didn't get half of what I had to offer. You would have done a lot better if you had been on the up-and-up.

Almost twenty years ago, I enthusiastically joined a co-op trying to market Butternut squash in a big-time way. The idea was solid. Most retirees from the Northeast migrated to Florida or some other warm climate for their declining years. At certain times of the year, they longed for home and for the things they enjoyed in their prime, i.e., Butternut squash for Thanksgiving and Christmas. The problem was it doesn't grow that well down south and it doesn't taste the same when it does. And another big thing: as arthritis sets into aging hands, peeling these reminders of home becomes nigh on impossible.

Ah-ha, a marketing opportunity. A co-op was formed and as a founding member, I put in a considerable amount of money. A study was done and we were off to the races. The basic idea was sound, though the abilities of the ruling body inadequate. It ended up folding largely because it failed to understand the scope of what it was attempting to do. With manual labor alone we were trying to accomplish what needed industrial strength. It could not work. The basic principle of, "If it can be done by a machine, it must be done by a machine," had never been thought about, much less employed. "Water over the dam."

I lost a lot of money, and so did many others. I was never paid a nickel for any of the many acres of squash I raised and harvested for this entity. But one stroke of luck did pay off for me. Taft Farms was all-in for this effort, even to the point we rented additional land to grow the product. My neighbor, Lou,

had health problems, but we had always had a neighborly relationship. He might have been confined to the hospital, but he
wanted his land to be farmed for at least one more season, the
years catching up to him. Eagerly we plowed up and planted the
extra thirty acres, hoping to share some of the return with its
rightful owner, but it was not a good year. The lowland did okay
but the upper portion suffered from a lack of water. We were
able to irrigate our farm, but the upland of Lou's place next door
was out of the question when it came to additional water.

The lowland produced, more or less, what was expected. On
the upland the yield was small and rather poor quality. But just
like with the pumpkins there was one exception. I make a practice of walking my fields from time to time during the growing
season just to see what is going on. I had spotted this particular
plant long before harvest, noting the way it seemed to thrive
when all around it suffered. It set fruit and continued to set fruit
long after its neighbors had given up. Drought conditions
seemed to have no effect on this particular plant, which also appeared to have fruit a little darker in color than its neighbors.

Before the harvest crew reached this area, I picked all sixteen
squash (wow) produced by this single plant and brought them
to my home. My mother-in-law, who lived with us and fixed
many of our meals since both Martha and I were working, was
given instructions to save whatever seeds she found in preparing
this squash. I was not prepared for what she found.

The flesh was much darker than the normal Butternut
squash, and it needed no additional sweeteners; it was already
much sweeter than any other squash. It was incredibly sweet. I
paid a lot more attention to this squash, the co-op having since
failed and out of the picture as far as revenue stream was concerned. Though it seemed to have a few irregularly shaped fruit,
the flavor, sugar, seemed consistent. We had no doubt concerning its drought-resistance but what we hadn't counted on was
its ability to produce almost thirty percent more product than
the standard of the industry, Waltham Butternut. Something
else became apparent, almost by accident. It had a great deal of

resistance if not immunity to many of the common diseases affecting Butternut squash.

I've come close to losing this strain on more than one occasion, whether by carelessness or other reasons, but we still have it and it has not been compromised with any seed company. Perhaps one of my sons will finally realize the value of what I have fought to save, though sometimes I think they feel I'm nothing but an old fool.

They might be right. Always looking for an edge in marketing I tried raising wheat a few years ago with the idea of saying, "We grow the grain, we grind the flour, we bake the bread." I felt this would be an irresistible edge in marketing our homemade bread. To many it was. I remember one person in particular looking me right in the eye and replying, "How quaint."

I wasn't quite prepared for this response. Apparently, she saw nothing out of the ordinary. "Wonder-bread" was just as good in her mind.

Wheat is just one of those grains we grow as a cover crop for the fields over winter. The idea of harvesting it as a grain and marketing it as a homemade bread was only an afterthought, something that came about after the needs for re-seeding to help the land. It might be a nice thought but hardly something practical or with any economic value, given the current price of grain.

The difference was I walk my fields from time to time, and I see things a grower with thousands of acres never notices. Wheat has four rows of seeds on its head, everyone knows this, it's not rocket science. I found one single plant in a field of roughly four acres with six rows of seeds. What does this mean? Not much, especially in view of the "mega-acres" grown across the heartland of this country. I have tried over many years to get this trait to replicate itself but with only moderate success. I often wonder just how many superior strains of whatever crop go un-noticed only because the scale is so large, the unusual simply went by the boards. Small-scale farming might have seen something with possible mega-effects if someone had only noticed. I don't think too many modern crops were domesticated from the wild by agri-giant corporations fifty thousand years ago. It was all done by small, subsistence farmers trying to improve what they grew to feed their families.

All of today's modern corn, or as it is called almost everywhere else in the world, maize, is based on four common parents. A friend, a researcher from UMass, at one time told me he thought he had found a fifth while on a trip to Mexico. To the average person this means next to nothing but in the global context this is potentially enormous. To expand the available gene pool on a crop so important is beyond comprehension. I haven't heard any more from him or anyone else for that matter regarding his possible discovery. It's either taking a long time to confirm or it's not what he thought it was. In either case I applaud his efforts—someone has to do it, someone who is not simply motivated by making more monopolistic money for Monsanto. How's that for an appropriate alliteration.

The next revolutions in agriculture are going to come from small farmers, people with large home gardens and researchers at land grant universities who have no agenda in mind other than improving the food supply. Altruism does still exist.

• • •

Some years ago, we suffered a great flood just about the time the fall harvest was to begin. My son Keith was even featured on an ABC news piece as he picked pumpkins from a rowboat. The direct effects of the flood were devastating, but a side effect was most unusual. A row of trees kept many of the various pumpkins, squashes, and gourds from washing down the Housatonic River. A huge pile of them just rotted in place after the water lowered and their seeds germinated in place.

Mendel's law of genetics kept their fruit from being anything substantially different from their parents, but the best was yet to come. This giant compost pile of sorts produced an appreciable amount of saleable product. After the previous year's disaster, we gladly took advantage of it, but at the end of the sales season many pumpkins, squash, and gourds were left over. These were rather unceremoniously dumped at the end of one of the fields where they lay until the following spring. The wildlife feasted on them all winter long but come spring the remaining seeds were scattered throughout the area by an overly aggressive tractor operator preparing the land for a new planting.

As a result, weird looking squash and pumpkins kept coming up in whatever crop was supposed to be planted in the area. We finally gave up on trying to pull them all out, and they just grew. They were some of the strangest things I have ever seen. We sold most, our customers were thrilled, and we saved seeds from some of the most bizarre, some of which I am still cultivating today.

We still have what I call a Star Squash, one of the sweetest things I have ever tasted, and striped pumpkins of various sizes. Whenever a customer asks us the name of this variety, we reply, "Why, it's Mendel Squash." One guy even tried looking it up on the Internet and of course got nowhere. We call it Mendel Squash because it would probably take a mind like that of Gregor Mendel to figure out just what is in there.

Earlier I mentioned that most corn research is being done at laboratories, but some is also still being done down on the farm, our farm. Saving seeds for sweet corn is a no-brainer; it's just not worth it but I routinely save my own seed for the most remarkable ornamental corn you will ever see. Over more than fifty years we have carefully selected seeds to produce the most brilliantly colored, longest and largest ears anyone can imagine. Brokers who sell this kind of thing wholesale nationwide have approached me wanting to set up a deal of sorts, but to this date I have resisted because I do not want to have all my eggs in one basket. They all want to have an exclusive, but if you only have one customer for your product, you are in trouble.

In the meantime, I continue to develop the variety, which has a size of sometimes eighteen inches in length, a color range way beyond anything now on the market, and the ability to hold its color for months, many months. It does not seem to fade when exposed to continuous light. When the deal is right and the product is ready I, or my heirs, will let go of it, and the pumpkins, and the Star Squash, and the many other things we have been working on over the years. This time we will be a lot more careful than we were in the past. Who knows, maybe Mendel Squash will be what saves our farm.

Vicious Vegetables

Everyone has occasionally bitten into a fruit or vegetable that didn't taste quite as advertised, but have you ever been attacked? As preposterous as this may sound, the answer for me is an emphatic, "Yes."

I have popped ripe grapes into my mouth only to find a Yellow Jacket was hollowing one of them out in search of sugar. Have you ever been stung on your tongue? It's not pleasant, I assure you. Bees and wasps of various sorts are a regular hazard in farming (ask anyone who's run over a nest of ground bees while mowing grass), but it's the unexpected encounter in the illogical place that hurts the most.

In the later part of the summer season, we all have to be mindful of wasps in the sweet corn. They are not directly there for the sugar as their cousins the Yellow Jackets are with the grapes but rather for the aphids. In nature's world, prey must, by their very nature, vastly outnumber their predators. It also follows they have a much higher reproductive rate. During the bulk of the season, ladybugs (technically Ladybird Beetles) and other natural predators tend to keep the aphid population under control, but by late August either the aphid population has exploded or the usual cast of predators has lost interest. It is not unusual to see entire plants of any species covered with aphids. Enter, the wasp.

Wasps, like the Yellow Jackets, feed on sugar. They just obtain it in a different manner; they get it from eating aphids that suck the sweet juices from the corn. When picking sweet corn in late summer or early fall, my crew has to be wary of wasps on the ears. Most of the guys have been stung at least once, often in the early morning when the air is a bit cooler and the wasps are sluggish, not yet alert enough to fly away. Somehow, it's hard to think of them as beneficial insects while your painful hand is swollen like a balloon.

• • •

Corn, all corn, can get you in a way that you might least expect. On a very hot day, contact with the corn leaves can give you a rash almost as bad as poison ivy, not to mention cuts similar to paper cuts, just larger and deeper, from their leaves. If you happen to be wearing shorts or a short-sleeved shirt, the tender undersides of your arms or the inside of your thighs are the most vulnerable locations. The itch can seem intolerable and the pain from scratching hard to bear, but resist the temptation, for as soon as you wash yourself with plenty of fresh water the problem will go away. The cuts take a little longer to heal. For most the rash only comes once a season. It seems one can build a tolerance, though it fades once the exposure is gone.

• • •

Bees of any kind can be a hazard while picking fruit, though raspberries harbor stinging insects of all kinds, even large biting flies. The sweetness of the berry combined with a hot day can make for treacherous conditions. Raspberries also have thorns, tiny but very hard to remove from your finger. Most of my workers have enough callouses they don't think twice about them, but customers picking their own usually do not have the tough skin to avoid trouble. One woman insisted we call 911 for her finger.

• • •

Blackberries are another matter... they can be lethal. Most species of cacti don't have thorns to compare with that of black-berries. These guys are brutal; the only thing worse that comes to mind is Acacia in Africa, and blackberry thorns are all hooked in different directions. Long-sleeved shirts and long pants are essential if you plan to do anything in the immediate vicinity of blackberries. I swear, they reach out and grab you. If caught, whatever you do, don't try to pull yourself loose, for they'll only dig in deeper. You just have to be patient and systematically work yourself out of their grip. The rewards are worth it, but picking blackberries is not where you bring the kids for an af-ternoon adventure. There are thorn-less varieties, but they just won't grow around here.

• • •

We raise up to twenty kinds of hot peppers each year. The market has been increasing by leaps and bounds largely due to the influx of a Latino population. I have instructed my staff to always wear plastic gloves when picking. Some of the lesser-hot varieties are okay, poblano and jalapeño are a good example of mild, but many of the chili type can at least cause a rash as bad as the one given by the corn, and it doesn't have to be a hot day. The so-called "Scoville Scale" is a measure of just how hot a pep-per can be. For example, a jalapeño carries a designation of 18, while a Ghost Chili is rated at 1.3 million. The pickers wear gloves because the juice that will inevitably get on their hands is just as deadly as the pepper itself. Just wiping the sweat off your brow or trying to remove an insect that flew into your eye can mean a trip to the emergency room and a great deal of dis-comfort, that is if you don't go blind. Demand is there but one must always put safety first when dealing with something as dangerous as the really hot ones.

• • •

Tomatoes can cause a very itchy rash. For years, I thought the welts occasionally experienced were the result of some fungicide, but the rash was still affecting us even after we no longer used these sprays. One of my workers made an astute observation: certain varieties were far more likely to cause a rash than others. With our limited knowledge of the breeding process used in developing the varieties grown at the time, we could not establish a clear pattern. Even today, years later, when we mostly grow heirloom varieties, it is still a truism that certain plants are more likely to cause a problem. Tomatoes are a poisonous plant but apparently some are more poisonous, at least to the touch, than others.

• • •

Anyone can discover rather quickly that the many varieties of Zucchini and Summer Squash have thorns. These guys like to attack the underside of your arms as you reach inside the plant to pick them. This is such a problem that major seed companies have gone to great lengths to breed out the thorns. A few of the Zucchini varieties are advertised as "thorn-less," but it really means "less thorns." They still have their share. A middle-eastern variety of zucchini called "Coosa" has thorns in places where none should be. Demand for "Coosa" is borderline extreme. It is, without doubt, head and shoulders above any other type for flavor, often tasting like it was cooked in butter while only steamed. Everyone wants it, but no one wants to pick it. The thorns on this thing are somewhere between those of the blackberry and the Acacia mentioned before. Sorry—if I'm going to grow it, I've got to get a lot more for it than for the others, and no one wants to pick it.

• • •

Kids love to pick their own pumpkins and who can blame them? Halloween is probably second only to Christmas in a kid's mind. When we pick pumpkins for sale on the store, our pickers all wear leatherwork gloves. The stems on pumpkins can bite back. Most of the thorns are rather small and the leather gloves tend to rub them off, but when one of the uninitiated grabs hold of the perfect pumpkin in the field while bare-handed, the pumpkin fights back. A few problems happen every year despite warnings.

• • •

Perhaps one of the more bizarre incidents of plant attack happened to me personally about twenty years ago and still defies explanation.

We grew a considerable amount of carrots in those days, packaging and sending them off to stores and supermarkets as far away as Boston. Most of our harvesting was still being done by hand. We liked to think it was tender loving care—another way of saying it was backbreaking. I had already dug several beds, and the guys were picking them up behind the tractor. It was important we got them in to the processing area as soon as possible because if they dried in the field, they were much harder to wash clean. I parked the tractor and started helping the guys finish up, filling a couple of totes all by myself. There were only a few bins to go, but as I reached down to pick up a carrot, I felt a blinding pain in my right thumb. My thumbnail had been completely torn off. Bleeding like crazy and hurting I wanted to know what had caused this, but nothing out of the ordinary could be found. Two of the guys dug all around the area, examined all the carrots (sometimes they will grow around a sharp object), but nothing could be found.

As Ronnie, one of the workers, put it, "I guess you just got bit by a carrot."

Trucks, Part II

Snow plowing was a way to get through the winter. Stan and I both left the teaching profession in 1970 and needed something to pay the bills during the off months of the farm. Snow plowing and other ventures helped fill gaps in the income stream. An old Blue GMC pickup and a little Ford Bronco came to the rescue.

I know not how Stan acquired the Bronco. I've heard various stories from winning a bet to setting up a friend's ugly sister with a date. Truth is, it was probably just purchased, but it came with a small seven-foot snowplow.

The GMC was a high-sprung beast we got from a local gas company for a couple of hundred dollars. The plow was added later. Converted to carry heavy loads and pull an equipment trailer into almost inaccessible places, its oversized tires, oversized springs, and oversized frame made this workhorse a formidable beast. But it had been used and abused.

After using the Blue Beast for the better part of the summer on the farm, it was time to get it ready for plowing, but few of the lights seemed to work. Running it through corn and hayfields all summer had raised hell with the wiring. Repair seemed out of the question. It would be easier to just rewire, starting at the switches.

Headlights and taillights seemed to work fine. But if we were to be able to pass the required inspection, the signal and brake lights also had to work, and they did not. We must have checked the wiring twenty times, but the same problem persisted. No matter whether you wanted to turn left or right, both sides blinked alternately. One side was on, the other off. One side on, the other off. What the hell was going on?

Enter one Bob Hayden, the guru of auto electrics. He laughed, "You have bad grounds."

Because the truck was so rusted, none of the original fittings worked. We had to run ground-wires from each accessory to a solid part of the frame. We did it and everything worked like a charm.

Both had serious issues; the Bronco had canvas doors and top meant to come off in warmer weather for possible use on the beach. Okay, it was going to be a bit cold plowing snow, but the rest of the body was the real issue. Earlier owners had apparently run it on the beach, probably into the surf. Salt had taken its toll; body rot was its most noticeable feature, fenders almost non-existent. The rust was so bad that one day the summer before we plowed, I stopped to pick up a hitchhiker on my way to town. He took a look at the old Bronco and said, "No thanks." At least he didn't run screaming into the woods.

The GMC ran pretty well, especially for the price, but it had been beat on badly. Not a single sheet-metal portion of its body was without a dent. It had been repainted, mostly to hide the name of the company, but it was painfully obvious this truck did not have a long-term future. It was a bear. Heavy-duty had a new name but if looks could kill, this truck was already dead.

We were desperate. We had both given up the security of our teaching jobs and were on our own, and I had a young family. We had to hope for snow, lots of it.

The gods smiled on us, though maybe not on our customers. Record snowfall, well over a hundred inches, and no storm dumped more than ten. It was a snowplowing dream, and it got us through until spring with no breakdowns. Both trucks were in tough shape, but for some reason they both lasted, and we were able to survive to farm in the spring.

• • •

One of the things hardest for any layman to understand is that we *wanted to be farmers*. Both of us had worked at other jobs in the past and had left what some would call lucrative if not secure positions to come back to the land. Everything had to go right for us to survive. Mistakes were not an option, and I have to credit my late brother with having made most of the right decisions. Stan had the unique ability to see an opportunity before it became a trend and he seemed to know when to bail out just as it reached the top of the bell curve. Buying the right vehicle for the right purpose at the right time was a knack he possessed in spades. These largely beat-up old trucks had enough life left in them to get us over the hump to the point where we could finally afford something to make life a little easier. A little luck put us into position to take our version of a great leap forward.

The first big jump came with our purchase of a very used 1967 white diesel truck. This thing could easily handle twice the cargo of the old Chevy, but it was another learning curve figuring out how to drive it. A ten-speed transmission with a split-axle and Detroit 351 under the hood was way different from the four-speed Chevy. It took a while, but we eventually figured it out, and both of us received an advanced-class license for our efforts. At least five employees took advantage of the opportunity and received theirs as well, some still driving trucks today. The White took us all over the eastern part of the U.S., whether picking up or delivering. I personally took it to Ohio and New Jersey at least a few times a year. Stan took it even further afield.

The next truck to leave its print on the farm was a 1979 International 2500. Buying this behemoth (at least to us) with a refrigerated body signaled to the farming community that we had arrived. It seemed a thing of beauty; at least the imperfections were well hidden, and after the installation of the "pusher axle" its legal weight capacity went up to almost 60,000 pounds. I felt we could have loaded it with rocks and it wouldn't be overweight, but I came close a couple of times.

By this time, in the mid-'80s, we were probably the largest grower of potatoes in Berkshire County. I was regularly hauling full loads of Russet baking potatoes to brokers in Boston and returning with loads of out-of-season produce for the store.

Before the pusher axle was installed, our gross weight was somewhere around 40,000 pounds. I was on my way into the market when I was stopped by a state policeman.

"You wouldn't be just a little overweight, would you?" he asked.

"No, I don't think so," I replied.

"I don't have scales handy or I'd make you go across them, but I'd guess you're at least ten grand over. You know the fine is a dollar a pound. Let me see your license and registration, please."

I handed them over, dreading what would happen next.

He looked everything over carefully but never went back to his cruiser. "Well, it's a damn good thing you're a Polack like me," he said. "I don't want to see you out here again unless you're carrying a lot less or have another axle to support the load."

With that he walked away, and we survived what could have been the fine that put us out of business. The new axle was installed on the truck within the week.

I had no more trouble from the state police after the new axle. With our new capacity being obvious, they didn't even waste their time.

But the best was yet to come—Seed potatoes were another issue. I made trips up to northern Maine to get what many considered the best seed in the nation, but some of the varieties being offered in cooperation with Cornell University were too hard to resist. After consultation, I ordered what I thought would be another load, but I guessed wrong.

It was a little adventure. My wife decided to come along for the all-day trip to northern New York. First stop, right in the shadow of the ski jump at Lake Placid. We had been here for the Olympics in 1980. Just four pallets of what were supposed to be something special, and they were.

Next, off to Malone where the rest of the load was to be

picked up. The ride was nothing short of enjoyable, even in the truck. We were seeing things and places we would likely never see again. When we arrived at the farm, everything was ready. All we needed to do was back in and they would load up, and load up they did.

"What do you want to do with the other four pallets?" the foreman asked as we were having lunch with the farmer and his wife.

My desire had not considered the capacity of the truck, but we still had a card to play. There was still room between the top of the pallets and the roof of the truck. They pulled off the pallets and started hand stacking as high as they could go. Finally, they had to close one door and pile bags against it. At long last, every bag of seed-potatoes was aboard, but what did we weigh? Soon after getting on the Northway in Plattsburg, we found out.

The sign read, "State Police Weigh Station ahead. All trucks must stop." My heart dropped. According to our bills of lading, we were close. Very close.

They weigh your truck one axle at a time, but it seemed as though it was taking an unusually long time for the front.

"Move up so we can get the rear two together."

The trooper approached my window. "You were a little over in the front, but you had a few pounds to spare on the rear, but I wouldn't even stop for fuel if I were you. There's less than fifty pounds between you and a fine."

We made it home… barely, running on fumes, but at least paid no fines.

The International served us well for many years. Unfortunately, it was the rising cost of fuel that ended its journey and that of the White. I sold the White to a fellow who still uses it to haul concrete septic tanks. He mounted a crane on the chassis and passes the increased fuel costs along to his customers.

Detroit engines rarely die. They got their start in WWII as the power plants for the famous PT boats. Never known for economy, they never quit and had power to spare. Unfortunately, the International had an even larger version of the White's engine due to the increased weight capacity, but its economy was poor at best. At eight to ten miles per gallon unloaded and only four to five loaded, it was not something anyone could afford to drive. After having sat for years and only used for storage in that time, it was finally hauled away for scrap just this spring. I'm going to miss those trucks where I spent a lot of time behind the wheel.

Laurel and Hardy

Batman and Robin, Dean Martin and Jerry Lewis, George and Gracie—dynamic duos are more the rule than the exception. At the farm, we've had our share of duos, couples, pairs, and in some cases, direct opposites. Over the years we've had two sets of twins, numerous siblings, romances, and a few marriages. I even gave one bride away in a ceremony held in our greenhouse. I was as proud of her as if she was my daughter. She came into her own while at the farm. On more than one occasion I became her "father confessor, what should I do" person. Ten years later, her husband, also a good friend, and her two children were to embark on a special vacation to see the rest of the U.S.

Mostly, strong friendships evolved, and many of these former workers are still in touch with one another and with me at the farm. I always enjoy the visits.

Once in a while, unlikely pairings take place such as in the case of Mark and David. Dave impressed me the first time I saw him. He was big for his age, a strapping young man with impeccable manners, simply asking if there was a possibility of employment at the farm. Both my brother Stan and I agreed he was a good candidate. Intelligent, polite almost to a fault, this young man was what we needed to deal with sometimes irascible customers demanding immediate attention. He did not disappoint us.

Mark was another story altogether. When he first came in to apply, his father did all the talking, but one had to be impressed.

Mark was easily six-foot five and 250 pounds but appeared timid, but that was only in the beginning, the opposite of what came later. Both Stan and I were reluctant, but this guy was obviously one hell of a strong dude and could do just about anything we needed. If we ever needed a hired gun, he was it.

The two of them started about the same time and, believe it or not, became close friends. Their dynamic was reminiscent of the classic comedy team Stan Laurel and Oliver Hardy. Mark opened up after becoming more familiar with the surroundings, showing himself to be somewhat of a clown, "anything for a laugh, but I can back it up!" Dave announced he was trying to become a minister in the Baptist Church, but the two of them were close even though Mark more than once offered Dave a beer. Dave countered with graham crackers and soft drinks. Graham crackers don't go well with beer, of any kind, except maybe root beer.

The two of them got along well, famously well, despite their differences; maybe Dave was trying to make a convert, maybe Mark was trying to show Dave a good time? Who knows? They're still friends today, still polar opposites.

It seemed every other word out of Mark's mouth began with "F" and wasn't anything resembling "farm." Dave never uttered a foul word no matter the circumstance, and there were times when his patience was well tested, not by Mark but events beyond his control. He was one of the most even-tempered individuals I have ever met. Mark, on the other hand, could fly off the handle at a moment's notice, and occasionally I had to step into a situation before it got out of hand.

Dave kept reminding Mark he was going to burn in Hell unless he mended his ways. Mark said he thought he was already there; this was the farm, wasn't it? If Hell was where all the bad people went, why was Dave here? They would laugh it off and go pick corn or something. Later, they would pack up some of the younger kids and all go off to Riverside Amusement Park. Mark would have his beer and Dave his milk and crackers. The kids thought they were great and respected them both.

If there was work to be done (when isn't there on a farm?), I found that keeping the two of them together made for entertainment that made any task easier and faster. Despite their philosophical differences, they balanced each other well and jobs were completed faster and better. That was one of the best crews the farm has ever had.

I believe the real test came in '75 on a day that was one of the hottest and most miserable I can recall. Most of the picking for the day had been done in the cooler early morning hours, but after lunch there were still hours to go before the crew left. Heat and the oppressive humidity were brewing up violent thunderstorms to the west, and I couldn't see sending them back out into the field with a major storm on the way in. Clouds that had built for hours began to look ominous, but there was the chance the storm would pass off to the north; a lot of them did.

I decided to take advantage of the limited time and send the full crew to the barn, our potato storage, to tidy up and sanitize in anticipation of this year's crop. Potatoes were a major part of the farm's financial picture back then. Eighty-five acres of spuds were sold right through our store almost from one end of the season to the next. The storage had to be thoroughly sterilized before the next crop came in, just the thing for the next couple of hours.

Things progressed smoothly, but within the first hour it became obvious this storm, a bad one, was not going north. For those who remember, this was the one that spawned a tornado in West Stockbridge, killing four at the old Berkshire Truck Plaza. The next day we found pieces from the roof of the Truck Plaza in our cornfield. I was told by a friend at our local radio station that the tornado had indeed come over but stayed aloft, thank God.

I have personally never witnessed a more violent storm at any time, and the crew suspended work to gape in awe of what was happening just outside our huge overhead door. We all hung back a little because the lightning and wind were something to behold, but Dave stepped forward to the edge of the storm and, lifting his arms to the heavens, yelled at the top of his voice, "Praise the Lord!"

At that very moment, a bolt of lightning hit close by, I'm not sure just how close; maybe it struck the silo next to the door. Whether it was the force of the blast or a knee-jerk reaction on Dave's part, he fell backward and landed on the floor in a state of utter shock. I knelt down to see if he was okay, but he was too stunned to respond.

Mark, on the other hand, also leaned over but with a serious, almost menacing look and said calmly, "Dave, shut the fuck up."

Neither ever stepped out of character.

Sometimes We're Rather Uncouth

W e've always worked hard at the farm, and we often get so dirty my wife makes us strip outside the house before going directly to the shower. At one time she even proposed we install a "pre-cleaning place" outside. As grubby as we get, we never sit down to dinner without first making ourselves presentable. That's the rule.

I've often skipped lunch when I was in the middle of something judged more urgent than a growling stomach, but there have been times not pausing for a break would have been the worse option. Such was the case once back in the 1980s when my son and I were making a rather complex irrigation set on a field of potatoes.

The proper amount of water is an absolute necessity for raising quality potatoes. Once the fruit starts to set in the ground, it becomes essential for the plants to have at least one vertical inch of water per week. This may not sound like a difficult task but keep in mind an acre-inch of water is just over thirty thousand gallons, and sometimes it doesn't rain at all for several weeks.

Laying all the pipe, setting all the Big Guns and sprinklers, and running the various pumps is a considerable job, especially when it's well above the ninety-degree mark by 11 a.m.

The pipe had all been laid out the day before by another crew, so my son Keith and I set out to get everything hooked up. We knew it wouldn't be easy, especially in view of the forecast— unmerciful heat—so we got a start right at daybreak. It seemed to take a little longer than normal to get the pump hooked up, for we had a hard time locating a deep enough pool in the river to draw from. We hadn't had substantial rainfall for several weeks, adequate for the early growth but not enough now that fruit-set had started. The river was low.

Once the pump was properly situated and anchored, draft lines established it was time to tackle the field. One at a time, the forty-foot sections of eight-inch pipe had to be joined. They felt extra-heavy and unwieldy, and we would have both sweated a great deal even if the temperature had not reached the ninety-degree mark. It was well in excess, but we didn't know it at the time.

Sweaty, dirty, grimy, throw in greasy from having to work on the pump, we were in rather tough shape by any civilized standard. I don't think either of us wanted to get too close to one another for the smell, but were both more than a little hungry when it came noon and neither of us wanted to have to get cleaned up for lunch only to get even worse after and then repeat the process. We both had eaten a substantial breakfast earlier, but it was gone. We needed refueling.

Whenever I know I'm going to be doing something gross, I remove anything of value from my person. Now it is my cellphone, wallet, and usually my keys, but back then it was just my wallet. Since irrigation had been an ongoing thing for more than ten days now, my wallet had taken up permanent residence on the dashboard of one of the farm pickup trucks. I had forgotten all about it. I was the only one driving this truck, so there was little concern about security; besides, honesty was never a concern with the people who worked for me back then. Mark, my foreman, never took his wallet off the dashboard of the pickup he drove home.

A few days prior, friends of mine from the Entomology Department at UMass had set up pheromone traps on the farm. So isolated from other agriculture, we were regarded as having a very nearly virgin population of insects. None of our bugs were resistant to any pesticides; in fact, they were regarded as being little different from the day God conceived them. For this reason, they were needed to determine just how resistant populations of the same pests had become elsewhere. Only male moths could be captured in this manner, but since they were an indicator of the broader population, at least this was a start. The problem was the lures used to attract these insects, mostly moths, had to be replaced every few days. Could I help the researchers out and do this task? Of course, I could. They gave me an assortment of lure replacements, none much larger than a dime in size, which I put in my wallet for safekeeping, the wallet that had been on the dashboard of the pickup for the last several days.

Keith and I piled into the yellow pickup, the one with no plates, no inspection sticker, no muffler for that matter, and headed into town to Burger King. McDonald's was closer, but we both decided we liked the burgers better at Burger King; besides it was only a few hundred yards farther anyway. If a cop took exception to our vehicle, the distance would not have mattered.

Our dirty, yellow pickup, loaded with odd-looking aluminum fittings and sounding like it might not live to go any farther pulled into the lot. I'm sure we smelled, and I know we were dirty, so dirty we probably left a trail behind us as we walked. Visitors from the city wondered which rock we had just crawled out from under. My mother had a saying that best summed it up. We looked like something only a mother could love, but it had to be a payday.

I carried my wallet in my hand; I was so grungy I didn't want to risk putting it in my pocket but we both got a chuckle as we passed a poster advertising a new kind of chicken sandwich being offered. The poster had the word "Incredible" splashed across it in giant letters, except someone had covered over the "C" and "R" with duct tape and now it read "In-edible." Pranksters rule.

Fortunately, there was no line to place orders—no one would have wanted to be anywhere near us and I'm sure the staff did their best to clear us out as quickly as possible, but we still had to pay and we did not look like we were dressed for the ball. Keith ordered and so did I, and then it was time to pay.

The cashier was a girl who had worked for us at one time and knew how dirty we could get on the farm, but I apologized for our appearance and assured her we would leave as soon as we received our orders. She laughed and said it was all right. Many workmen of all trades came in and were often less than presentable.

We all burst out in laughter when I opened my wallet to pay her and no less than a dozen moths flew out. The lures had done their job, unfortunately at my expense. At least a dozen more just waited for me to disturb them before taking flight though still staying in my general vicinity.

Keith laughed as he swatted at them, further drawing attention to my predicament, and several moths followed me as we left the restaurant. I have never felt more like a yokel in my life.

The counter girl could not contain her laughter, patrons joining in. There wasn't a damn thing I could do, for the moths hung around me like I was their favorite candle. The burgers couldn't come fast enough. The whole scene had become a spectacle, as even I had to swat to keep them from landing on my face or eyeglasses.

I swear the burgers took longer in coming, and the whole restaurant was having too much fun at my expense. When the burgers finally arrived, we left with a small cloud following. I felt like the character from *L'il Abner* that always had a storm cloud over his head, only my cloud was moths.

No one has ever let me off that hook, especially Keith. The Burger King is now a Japanese restaurant, but thirty years later the story still gets a laugh, at my expense. I chuckle every time I hear it, sometimes with a new wrinkle or two. The whole thing was so ludicrous; no way anyone could have made it up.

The Mob

It was 2:30 in the morning in the year 2002, and my home phone was ringing off the hook.

"Hello, this is Officer Bersaw of the police. Your barn is on fire. The fire personnel are already there but don't rush. It's already lost."

That was pretty much the whole of it. I notified my wife and two sons and dressed as fast as I could, but one glance out the hallway window in the direction of the farm told me all I needed to know. It was gone. The sky was aglow with flames.

The old building built in 1809 had withstood hurricanes, blizzards, high winds, any and all sorts of calamities, including at least two other fires, but now it was gone. A monument to colonial-era engineering, it had boasted drive-in entrances on three of its five levels. So well constructed were its floors that it hardly creaked, even when a fully loaded tractor trailer backed in, and several had over the years. Frequently, during the potato harvest up to five ten-ton loads of bulk potatoes were parked on the third level to protect them from weather. Strong and durable are inadequate adjectives for describing the hand-hewn chestnut and fir beams in this building, now just smoking ruins.

Earlier the previous day, my son Paul had found a small fire and put it out. Baby chicks under a heating unit called a brooder had apparently dislodged a heating coil into the wood-shavings used as bedding and shavings ignited. Paul, who discovered it quite by accident, easily put out the small fire, more of a smolder. If it had not been for a softball game that caused him to leave the farm store earlier than normal, he might not have gone to feed the chicks until much later in the day. The fire would have been out of hand by then, but as luck had it, he was in time and shut off all power to the brooders. The chicks were old enough to no longer need the extra heat.

After notifying me, he went on to his game. Later, I went to the barn and did a double check. The burnt spot, about a foot in diameter, was wet and cold. I checked it with my hand; the fire was out.

As Paul and I rode to the fire in my pickup, we both decided to let the police and fire officials do their work. We would say nothing until the authorities determined how the fire started. We both knew where it did not start. All power had been shut off! Later, something rather obvious dawned on me: How does a one-ounce baby chick pull a glowing heat coil loose from its insulators and bury it in the wood shavings? The fire he found that afternoon had to have been someone's attempt at making the whole thing look like an accident.

Within hours of daylight, it was determined the fire was arson and had started more than forty feet from the baby chicks, magnesium permanganate suspected as an accelerant. Once arson was determined, Paul and I both explained what had happened earlier. We were chastised for not having said something sooner, but we had agreed it was better not to taint the investigation toward a foregone conclusion. But now authorities had to proceed in a different direction.

The historical status of the barn caught the notice of news organizations. All the local television stations came out to get pictures. A blurb even ran under a talking head on CNN. Calls of support came in from friends and business associates, and as soon as the word got out about this being a case of arson, the finger pointing began.

I had been involved in a controversial land transaction where a local citizen's group sought to prevent a developer from building high-end luxury homes on farmland. The group sought to prevent the construction by purchasing the property and keeping it in agriculture. I agreed to work with them; I was the agriculture. Less than a week after they succeeded in making the purchase, my barn burned.

Pardon the pun but no smoking gun was ever found. After a reasonable amount of digging and my even hiring a private investigator, I am more than ninety percent sure who set the fire and who paid him to do it. I even found, although I have not personally spoken with him, an eyewitness, but not one who would or could stand up in court. In short, just not enough evidence existed to bring anyone to trial.

• • •

If there is anyone who does not believe organized crime is involved in the produce business, I have a surprise for you: The "Easter Bunny" is waiting for you just around the corner. Please say hello for me. I have personally witnessed a dumpy little fellow with a large cigar accepting fat envelopes from brokers on the Boston Market. Of course, he was accompanied by two huge gorillas, probably ex-NFL linemen. As he went up the dock, every broker handed him an envelope, one would have to assume to make sure no problems descended upon their establishments.

The smaller regional markets were in all probability not exempted from the practice, but I never personally witnessed any behavior that could point otherwise. We assumed it was there.

I had met Ace before and been startled by his appearance. There were few words appropriate to describe him other than the single biggest human being I had seen to date. Seven feet tall, probably a little more, and well over four hundred pounds in weight, he was intimidating, to say the least. I once played football on a major collegiate level and I have to say, I have never encountered a bigger human specimen.

As you might suspect, Ace was afraid of no one and nothing. I always treated him with respect and he always looked kindly at me. Thank God. It was rumored he was the enforcer for the

Mob in the Albany area and few would doubt his efficacy in this capacity. If this guy said you had to pay up, you would sell your own mother into prostitution to keep him away.

I never had any problems with Ace; in fact, he was kind of a mentor. When I told him we were making pizza at our farm, he gave me many tips, mostly who I should pay off so I could get a contract to supply the public schools in my area.

"That's how you make the real money in pizza," he said. "Selling it to the public is crazy. Sell it to the schools. The kids eat it. Then the public pays you. That's how you make money."

He may have been right, but hopefully what we did wasn't all that wrong. I'm convinced he did know all the right people. He was not a poor man and he always did well by his friends, however you might categorize friendship.

Shortly after the fire, I went to the Menands (Albany) market to pick up needed items. All the brokers and farmers wanted to hear the story and I was obliged to tell it, of course, leaving out names. It took longer than normal to complete my transactions, the buying done first, the pickup later. Fortunately, these guys were all friends and I didn't have to repeat the story more than a few times. Finally, it was time to load-up. I was already more than an hour late, but I had plenty of help.

I was walking across the square to where my truck was parked when a custom van pulled up alongside. At first, I didn't recognize Ace. I never knew how he got to the market because he was always there, a friend of one of the best men I have ever had the privilege of knowing, Frank Esposito. "Espo" was single-handedly responsible for more people being in business and staying in business than any other person on the face of the earth. He extended credit to more people than any bank I know, and to my knowledge never made a mistake. For more than sixty years, Frank did business on a handshake and never regretted it. Maybe Ace was Frank's enforcer. I don't know, but I deeply loved them both.

"Hey, Taff. Hey, Taff!" Ace always sounded the role as well as fit the appearance. "I hear you got a guy over there that needs to find out who his friends are."

I always liked Ace and fortunately he always liked me. Though I had no idea what was happening, you had to be stupid not to know he was making me some kind of offer. "What are you talking about, Ace?"

"Taff, you're a good guy. You deal with all the right people. You pay your bills. The right people like you and somebody's done you wrong. This guy's got to find out who his friends are."

I could smell there was something wrong but had to plead ignorance. "Just what are you saying, Ace?"

"Look, some guys I know want to help you out, and maybe you will help us out when we need a favor. This asshole just needs to find out who his friends are, if he has any."

This was a we-help-you-you-help-us arrangement. I just had to know the details before going any further. "Just what do you mean, Ace?"

"Look, he needs to find out who his friends are. If you can't wipe your ass because both your arms are broke, someone has to do it for you, or you're gonna smell. You find out who your friends are. By the way, in case my friends need it, do you happen to own a backhoe in case we need to bury some garbage?"

I declined with a smile. He knew I was reluctant, but he told me the offer was open any time I might change my mind.

"We look out for good people who need a hand once in a while," he said. "The law only protects them that pay to have it made. We take care of problems what falls between the cracks."

The logic of what Ace said to me that day is irrefutable. It's obvious the ones with money and influence, whether on a local or national level, are going to get things their way. The rest of us just endure and fill those little cogs in the wheel to make the wealthy even wealthier. I admit, there have been times when I wondered what might have transpired if I had taken Ace up on his offer. Sadly, I will never know. Ace died from a massive heart attack a little more than a month after our conversation.

I'm not ashamed to say I miss him and his connection to a world where justice is metered out not according to how slick your lawyer is but rather by whether you are a decent player of the game. People seem to forget that organized crime sprung not from a desire for money or power but rather to find justice where none existed. Some have told me that Ace was all bluff and little substance.

The number of friends of all shapes and sizes, custom-made suits worn by very large men extending their condolences to his family, said otherwise.

They Don't Have a Clue

M uch has been said of the disconnect between those of the One Percent class and the rest of us. Sociologists, politicians, social workers, and others with at least a reasonable degree of perception have all decried the widening gap between those that have more than they can ever spend but still seek more and the rest of us just trying to stay alive.

I've been called stupid, ignorant, or just plain lazy because I chose not to go to the city to make my fortune. There have been opportunities, some of them lucrative and tempting, but I chose to stay here because I tend to value what I have more than what I might have had, because the life my children and now their children are having is built upon what I know is solid, not measured in terms of greenbacks but rather green.

I'm sorry if sometimes it seems I can't get off my high horse, but I recently had an encounter with a group of "Nouveau riche" that set me off, further reinforcing my belief there is something fundamentally wrong with our system.

Those of "old money" seem to have an appreciation for the masses that still work with their hands, who strive to overcome adversity, and who, in some cases, feed fat asses, whether or not they deserve it. One gentleman and his wife, multi-billionaires, have offered to loan me whatever I need to fix what the latest natural disasters have done to my farm. More than once, I have sat around the kitchen table with him and his wife over a couple of drinks. They are real people. They just have a lot more money than most but tend to use it where it will benefit more than just themselves.

But I know where my bread is buttered and must, by necessity, play the game, whether or not I like the rules. I once heard it said you follow the golden rule: "Them that have the gold make the rules." So it flows with Tanglewood, the music center for the Boston Symphony Orchestra. Not many families struggling to make ends meet are listed on the high rollers page of the program. We give the festival and its programs our full support, not only because they help "butter our bread," but because we believe in what they do and like to think we can appreciate the culture and art they help provide to an area that is often defined by its relationship with the arts. I really like good music. I think most of us do.

As a friend of Tanglewood and a major supplier to the caterers who wine and dine the big bucks, Taft Farms was invited to set up a table and display wares at the annual wine and cheese festival. We were grateful for the gesture because it was an opportunity to showcase our offerings to many of the coveted visitors, not all of who were familiar with our farm.

The table was successful beyond our wildest expectations. Both Pennie and Jim were veterans of the food show wars and the diminutive dessert doll. Julie blew away the competition by attracting crowds of sometimes wild-eyed patrons. During the break, other vendors mobbed our table in search of secrets. So successful was this venture into the stratosphere that Claudia, the gal at least nominally in charge, gave our group tickets to the "after-party party." It all sounded a bit strange but the way it worked was that first there came the Wine and Cheese Festival. Then the vendors got together for another party. The tickets given to us were for the party taking place after the second party, one for *very* special guests only.

No one from the farm had any idea what this event might be, but my son Paul gratefully accepted and then noticed the purchase price of two hundred dollars each. They had given us four of them… This was a special gift indeed.

Intimidated I'm sure, no one else from the farm wanted to be a part of something they felt was way above their heads, but after having accepted the invitation we had to make an appearance. Martha and I—senior statesmen, if you will—decided to be the "social guinea pigs".

We rushed like crazy to get ready.

"How do I look, honey? Am I overdressed?"

"How the hell do I know? I'm wearing slacks and a sport shirt. If they need a tux, I'm out of there."

The event was to be held at some estate I'd never heard of, not as if I've been invited to that many. Google couldn't find it, though there were several with similar sounding names, the most promising by description in Indiana... fat chance.

We drove on up to the parent site, Tanglewood.

"These are definitely Tanglewood tickets," the guard at the gate said. "I have no idea what they are but judging from the price it's gotta be special. You best check in with the man up there. He might know something more. These aren't anything like I've ever seen. I'll have to find out from the office. I have no idea where this is. You just wait here. I'll be right back."

Martha and I parked our rusty Toyota on the side and waited for the man to return. "Well, we're presentable enough. Maybe we should just take advantage of the opportunity and go out for a quiet dinner somewhere. Lord knows it's been a while. Summer means a seven-day work schedule."

He returned. "Wow, do you realize what you have here? These are the 'Gold Standard' of Tanglewood tickets. Influential people would kill for these. Only two hundred are issued."

"Hey, I'm a farmer, what do I know?" I replied. "Where the hell is this place?"

He gave directions; it wasn't far and we weren't that late; others arrived later than us. In social circles, I guess it's called "fashionably late."

A "Rent-a-cop" checked our tickets and helped find a suitable spot for the rusty Toyota alongside a Ferrari and a BMW. I was beginning to think we might be the skunks at someone's lawn party, but I'd try to put on a good face. Martha was well dressed and my gray hair might pass as distinguished if I played my cards right.

Everyone was friendly enough, not that I recognized a single face. We were neither overdressed nor under—it was completely informal, and we are not made to feel unwelcome or unworthy in the least. A gentleman who appeared to be in charge welcomed us (I never did catch his name) and directed us to a table of red wines. A similar table of white and another of blush were in another room.

"Don't just take a glass, take the bottle," he instructed. "Our job is to finish off all the open sample bottles from the earlier festival. The food will be out shortly."

Did the man say food? A twenty-foot-long span was soon laid out, containing dishes I cannot name plus a whole roast suckling pig, a steamship round of beef and several platters of stuffed baby quail, and more was coming later.

We gratefully took reasonably portioned plates and a bottle of Merlot to a spot out on the rear deck of this well-appointed but not ostentatious home. Martha and I were starved. It was now nearly nine and neither of us had had more than a stolen bite since breakfast. It was just the nature of the way things were at the farm in the busy season, and we were ravenous.

Eavesdropping is not intentional, just what happens when close by. It's unavoidable, especially if the participants are lubricated from wine all afternoon and perhaps speaking louder than normal. The overheard conversation went something like this:

"I just sold ninety percent of my holdings in Blank Corporation. If I need to, I can live off the dividends from the remaining shares, but an opportunity may come up for me to purchase a minority share in the Yankees. I may just exercise the option but a good-sized parcel of industrial land in Brazil looks attractive, just came on the market. My broker jumped on it and put down a small deposit to tie it up just in case. Got a good price for the shares, though, just a little over four hundred million; gonna have to do something with the money."

"Sounds like a good move, either way. I've been buying up underwater real estate in hot markets to hold until prices improve. I'm going to keep the best ones for last and sell the others as soon as I can return a decent profit. A lotta good deals out there but you need to stay away from anything cheap. I've instructed my buyer to not go for anything unless it's at least seven figures. Anything less usually needs work before you can sell it, and I'm looking at another vineyard in France. It's a good one with excellent product and a long history, and it turns a consistent small profit. It just needs better marketing here in the States."

Another voice chimed in, "Vineyards that turn a profit are rare in France. I picked up five more, two of them big ones, in Argentina and Chile. They are always profitable, mostly because the labor is so much less. The wine is good, but the costs are lower. We don't need to get big bucks for it to make money. My biggest problem is travelling down there so many times a year to keep tabs on things. Even the best managers will steal you blind or go soft on the help unless you keep them on their toes."

About this time, the speakers noticed Martha and me standing nearby on the porch. Politely, one asked, "What do you folks do?"

"Oh, we run Taft Farms down in Great Barrington," I answered.

"You people had a great display," replied the fellow who owned the vineyards in South America. "Well done, very professional; you must do a lot of these shows."

The others nodded in approval.

"Actually, very few. This was our first in a long time, but our people who staffed it are long-time pros. They know what they are doing."

"I'll say," replied the four-hundred-million-dollar man. "There were crowds at your booth all day. Job well done."

"So, how are things on the farm? Are the crops growing alright?" asked the South American vineyard man.

"They're growing fine. It just seems that about the time we are ready to start harvest Mother Nature throws us a curve ball. The day we started picking strawberries, three inches of hail laid waste to the field—the third time in a row it's happened. Freaky weather is raising havoc around here."

"You know, there is something to that. It seems I always lose one of my vineyards in France to some event every year. I hate it when that happens."

I made no reply, but I think he got the message. For him, the vineyards were a hobby, a rich man's toy, not something he depended on for his living. For us, a bad weather event could mean life or death, threaten our very survival.

Martha and I engaged in few conversations while there. We partook of the fancy fare we might never encounter again. The foie gras with truffles was different. If I had to rely on it to survive, I would probably starve; the portions were tiny, but the dish likely cost enough to feed a small town. Most of the evening we continued to catch snippets of conversation, a glance through a window, if you will, at a world we only hear about on the news or read about in the society pages.

Among the men, cars were a big topic, as you might expect. Whether or not the new Corvette could match up to Ferrari was discussed for some time. Vintage collectors bragged of their recent acquisitions, a Bugatti, an early Mercedes, or something previously owned by a celebrity. Oddly, I heard little discussion of sports.

Women spoke of vacations, islands they had visited, restaurants both domestic and foreign. One spoke of the new language she was learning in order to take a special trip to a seldom-visited faraway place I had never heard of. Reading and occasionally writing added to the feminine mix. Plastic surgery also came up, always what another woman had done and whether it had worked. Usually not.

Finally, near the end of the evening, we met one person with whom I was acquainted, a former classmate from Boston College named Jim who now owns and operates a high-end restaurant in Lenox. Jim shook his head as he overheard the conversations and partook of the fare. He and his wife are like Martha and me, from humble beginnings. "Just smile," he said, "And take what they offer and charge like hell for what they want. They can afford it."

Martha and I left shortly after and climbed into the rusty Toyota, the one with the door handle missing from the driver's side. We edged ourselves out from between the gleaming vehicles, each of which probably cost more than I make in not one but several years, waved goodbye to the rent-a-cop, and rattled on down the driveway, back to a completely different world.

The world of the rich is a nice place to visit, but I don't think I want to live there. It struck me as being all too phony and avaricious, even if somehow necessary to our lives here in the Berkshires.

Trucks, Part III

There were many trucks with personality at the farm. We had something called a Chevy "Hi-cube van." Basically, a three-quarter-ton pickup with a taller-than-normal body, it was great to deliver product in the local area, but my God was it noisy. The engineers who designed it never really gave any thought to passenger comfort. This thing rattled and squeaked from every angle. It did the job, but at a price: the sanity of the driver.

I once picked up a kid headed toward Great Barrington. When I left the curb, the noise started and he looked to the rear as if the whole truck was going to fall apart, him with it.

"We rent it out to the CIA on weekends," I said. "They can get away with saying it's not torture as defined by the Geneva Convention." He nodded and covered his ears with his hands.

"I can get out anywhere."

I barely heard him.

• • •

We still have the Mitsubishi. Though it's officially off the road we still use it from time to time, and it's not bad, just not reliable.

It coming into our hands came as a direct result of not being able to afford to run the International. E-Bay has a unique feature: If you are interested in buying a product—a vehicle, especially—you can have someone in the local area check it out to make sure it's not just a piece of junk.

Paul, my youngest son, located a truck in San Diego that seemed to fit the bill for what we wanted. An independent mechanic confirmed the score. We agreed on a price and soon my other son, Keith, and I booked tickets to the West Coast.

One problem: this was only a few months after 9/11. Two men with one-way tickets to the West Coast carrying a box of tools… oh, boy, was this suspicious or what? We were scrutinized, searched, and examined every step of the way. We co-operated with everyone, but it seemed tedious and repetitious. Despite arriving almost two hours earlier than necessary, we barely made our flight, but then the real adventure began.

The appropriate people met us at the airport, we completed the deal on the truck, and we retired in our motel for the evening, the odyssey to begin in the morning. Neither of us slept much, adventure at hand, but the fates had other ideas.

Everything was new, and we drank it in like fish. The roads were ten lanes wide, houses perched on what seemed impossible hills, fields of strawberries (all on plastic), places where wildfires had burned forever, and traffic. My God, I never knew there were so many cars in the world, but it all came to an abrupt halt when a loose drain-plug fell out of the engine on I-15. We nursed the cripple into a rest area in Temecula and made the calls. We were able to cancel the sale under the "lemon laws," get our money back, and arrange for a tow, but it took almost eight hours.

We were about as far away from home as we could get, with no reservations for either a motel or a flight back home, and we had no truck. The motel was easy, but we had to think fast. Things were not going our way.

We had the money from the return of the truck in cash. Don't ask. Even though we had paid by certified check, the original owner insisted on giving us cash. I was not in a position to question where it came from, and maybe I really didn't want to know. We still had to get home and needed a medium duty truck. We started shopping.

The owner of the original truck said he felt so badly about our predicament that he would gladly give us the refrigerated body if we could find another chassis that met our needs. We did, and after two more days of waiting for the body to be mounted and all the final details, we were once again ready to leave on our cross-country odyssey, but first we needed plates.

I was in the process of attaching farm plates from Massachusetts when the dealer exploded on me. "Are you completely nuts?" he shouted. "This is California. You'll be stopped every hundred yards and searched, accused of bringing some exotic pest into the state to wreak havoc on our farmers. Hide those goddam things before they get you killed."

For fifteen dollars he set us up with something called a One Trip Permit, a sticker that allowed us to travel anywhere in the continental U.S., but only once. Where we were going was noted on the sticker and we were given ten days to get there, but no plates. I wondered just how many times we would be stopped.

Finally, with a full tank of fuel and a desire to just get the hell out of San Diego, we left on a Friday on the first leg, about a ten-hour ride across the desert to Las Vegas. The trip was not without incident.

California gives new meaning to the idea of traffic. It seems it's always bumper-to-bumper, whether it's at a dead standstill or eighty miles-an-hour. Nerve wracking is the best way to describe eight lanes in each direction with every driver needing a Valium.

Exhausted as we were, we had to get going, and Vegas had just enough of an allure to egg us on, but it also called out to just about every other resident of San Diego. This was Friday; a weekend in Vegas. And none of them could get there fast enough.

I had the Mitsubishi floored but cars were passing us waving the familiar one-fingered salute. "I'm giving you all she's got, Captain." Then it happened: our throttle line broke loose and the engine suddenly dropped down to an idle. Fortunately, we were in the right-hand lane, but the breakdown lane was next to non-existent; it would have to do while we made emergency repairs. Our tools were in the rear, but there was no way to get there without getting killed. The multi-tool on my belt would have to do until we reached a safe rest area. Eighteen-wheelers rushed by just inches from me as I worked under the hood, but I was able to see what had happened and fix it, at least partially. Two more white-knuckle miles up the road we safely pulled off and re-trieved the tools from the back. It didn't take me five minutes to make proper repairs with the right tools. A quick unloading of over-stressed bladders and a fill-up and we were on the road again. Vegas here we come, hopefully with no more emergencies.

The vegetation of southern California gave way to the high desert. I was passing a trailer load of horses, one of the few times I passed anything. Keith was trying to catch a little snooze with his head almost out the window when a horse from the van stuck its head out and gave a loud snort into his ear. His reaction was as if he had been attacked by an alien.

"No Gas, Next 180 Miles," the sign read. That means it was just a rip-off, I figured. "No Gas or Diesel, Next 180 Miles. Check Your Gauge. We're Not Kidding!" We stopped and topped off the tank, just in case, and it did cost a lot more than it should have but they were right, there was no gas or diesel for the next 180 miles.

Las Vegas at night viewed from the I-15 overpass is a sight to behold. I never knew there could be so many lights in one place. The main hotel-casino strip is really not large, but the sheer number of lights is incredible. I can only imagine the size of the cables feeding them. There's a reason why they call this the biggest little city in the world.

We found a motel in north Vegas that didn't mind truckers, or farmers for that matter, and we both collapsed for the night, but not until I had an adventure with Mexican food. I thought they were julienne beans. No, they were jalapeño peppers, with something else added as well. The beer was excellent, a micro-brew I'd never tasted before. It helped reduce the flames.

I-15 eventually met up with I-70 in Utah but not before an-other adventure of sorts. For almost a mile (we slowed consid-erably to keep the picture), a bald eagle flew less than fifty feet in front of us. I'd never had the opportunity to see one in flight for more than a few seconds before. I'm sure he (or she) knew we were watching and just paced ahead of us for the whole distance. There was no way in hell I was going to give this bird any grief and it seemed to be able to read my mind. Giving a loud scream, it peeled off to the right. Whether in understanding or salute, I'll take it. There are times you can feel as one with the world. This was one of those moments.

Utah has places that boggle the mind in appearance. Not long after we passed a sign announcing that we had entered Zion National Park, the scenery changed dramatically. It seemed the only more or less normal paved road was between bridges over picturesque canyons. The sun was setting behind us and the red rocks took on a color of their own. I was driving at the time, and when I noticed a place to pull off, a scenic overlook, there was simply no way to resist. I'll never forget the look on Keith's face as he looked out at the chimney rocks glowing in the waning rays of sunlight. He looked at me and said, "There's nothing like this back home." I wished we could have stayed longer but we still had a long way to go before reaching his sister's place in Colorado.

We managed to make it to Vail, to my daughter and son-in-law's place, before the witching hour. Fortunately, I had been there before so I could find it even after dark. No jalapeño peppers masquerading as beans, no problems with the throttle, no eagles flying in front of the truck; we were in somewhat familiar territory, at least for me. For Keith, it was all new. Even the breathing was different at over eight thousand feet. But here it was cold, unlike the California and Nevada climate we had come from. Chris and Alex did their best to entertain us in the short time we could spend, showing the incredibly trendy Vail in its best light. I'll never forget the sight of three couples coming toward us in downtown Vail. Forget what the men were wearing, probably Men's Warehouse or at best, Brooks Brothers. Two of the women were in mink and the other was in sable. I recognized the sable because I had been to Siberia. You could have bought my farm and probably most of the town I live in for the cost of what those women were wearing. No anti-fur activists here. They can't afford to even visit. Poor people only work here. The rest don't care one way or another.

The next morning starting the diesel proved adventure enough. Even with below-zero temps and no plug-in available, somehow the Mitsubishi managed but it was close. After a considerable warm-up time we were off. Fortunately, the Eisenhower Tunnel under the Continental Divide was still open, though a storm was pending. At this altitude, almost twelve thousand feet, when a storm comes everything shuts down.

The descent into Denver was at the very least interesting. Signs kept reminding us that trucks had to use lower gears or else pull-off into designated areas until conditions improved. What did that mean? Spring? It was one hell of a downgrade, I can tell you. There are no foothills. Once you descend out of the Rockies you are on the Great Plains. I can only imagine what it must look like when coming from the other side. The Rocky Mountains just seem to rise from nowhere. One moment you are downshifting out of the mountains and the next you are on plains as flat as a pancake—in fact, flatter than a pancake. Colorado is best described as two different states: there are the mountains and then there are the plains. There's not much in between. As we sped across the flatlands, I could plainly see snow-capped mountains in my rear-view mirror. Crossing into Kansas was only a matter of a sign on the highway and, much in the manner of a used car sale, a used oil drilling rig sale. If you were lucky or you really knew what you were doing you could hit pay dirt at about thirty-five hundred feet. Is this your lucky day?

Vast distances between any form of civilization is the best way to describe Kansas. Our little Mitsubishi had limited fuel capacity and we were barely able to make it from one open facility to the next, but we did. We were just happy to be off the road for the night in a motel room when we heard the weather forecast, a snowstorm moving in rapidly from the west. Travel was going to be dicey at best.

We were up and out as early as possible, for we had to beat the storm as it came east. It caught up to us in Illinois, but not before we had the chance to cross the mighty Mississippi near St. Louis. Say what you will, it's a thrill, but we had to hunker down for the night; the storm had caught us and further travel was not permitted. Another motel, another night on the road, and maybe a chance to catch up between father and son. How about a steak dinner? Where else in the world could we expect to get a great steak than here?

Answer: almost anywhere. The whole place was a cloud of tobacco smoke. Smoking or non-smoking. Take your pick. You can smoke or not smoke. The choice is yours. A sort of blue cloud hung over the whole place while the TV blared something about contestants having to eat bull's testicles. The sign had said it was the home of the "World's Best Steak." Mine might have served better as a tire on the truck we were driving. Keith never finished his; the former defensive tackle said his steak was disgusting. The ambiance also left something to be desired, not exactly "world-class."

We let the storm pass, and in the morning set off on what we hoped would be the last leg of the journey. Numerous vehicles off the road proved we had made the right decision, but it was still a long way to Great Barrington.

It was after three in the morning when we finally rolled into Great Barrington. Barely alert, we passed a local cop waiting in a side street. I knew he gave us the look. There was no one else and he was probably bored. He pulled out to tail us, especially since we had no plates on the truck. Just outside of town his lights came on. We were less than two miles from home. After 3,100 miles of travel without any plates, a hometown cop threatened our legitimacy. Fortunately, the One Trip Permit from the state of California proved all was well. Five minutes later we were home, exhausted, odyssey ended.

We were lucky to have made it back. Within a month we had to replace all six of the tires. Though they had looked all right when we bought the truck, a closer inspection revealed they had all been re-grooved, and some of the grooves had cut through the outer layer of cords. Put any weight on it and the tires would blow. After pouring a couple of grand extra into the vehicle, we were actually able to get many years out of it, but it turned out to be not the deal we thought it was. When finally retired, it didn't owe us anything, but a father and his son had memories of a cross-country journey that would be hard to duplicate.

I had one other occasion where I took a one-way flight to pick up a truck, and not one on which I look back fondly. I received a call late one night from someone claiming to be my brother, only I could not recognize the voice. It was Stan, though he sounded like he was ninety years old. He was in a Veteran's Hospital in Florida, and he wasn't going to make it.

My sister and I hastily put ourselves together and headed to see him. By the time we arrived, he had already slipped into a coma from which he would never awaken, but by the time we had to leave he was still hanging on. That was a very hard goodbye. Almost two weeks later he passed. Every day we were there the doctors said he wouldn't last the night, but somehow, he kept going for a lot longer than anyone expected.

Before he lost his ability to do so, he gave specific instructions concerning his possessions. He gave me his Ford pickup and some tools and other items. After the highly emotional farewell, I headed north in the truck. Twenty-three hours and 1,300 miles later, I pulled into the farm. I stopped for nothing other than gas and a few snacks. There was no way I would have slept even if I tried. Expecting to get the bad news as soon as I pulled in, I was surprised not to. We even started to believe he might pull out, but he didn't.

Though it was only a two-wheel drive truck (they don't get much snow in Florida), it served me well for several years. It was a great over-the-road truck with many optional creature comforts I was not used to. When it finally died, it had a lot of miles on it, me putting as many on it as Stan had.

About the Author

Born during World War II, Dan Tawczynski lives in the house he called home as a child in Great Barrington, Massachusetts, the place to which his family migrated at the beginning of the twentieth century. Tawczynski graduated from Boston College where he met his wife, Martha. They have four children and seven grandchildren. Retired now, and fifty-four years of marriage later, they both still go to work at the farm store (Taft Farms, Inc.) each day, largely to help their son Paul, who now manages the business.

Tawczynski has always been a story teller of sorts. This is his first published work. If reasonably well-received, he has at least a hundred more shorts and recollections waiting, as well as many more still to be written.

Made in the USA
Columbia, SC
21 October 2021